Basil Bunting
a northern life

'A poet is just a poet, but I am a Northumbrian man.
It has always been my home, even when I've been living elsewhere.'

Basil Bunting, *Out Loud*, **The Listener** 94 (28 August 1975).

Tyne river view at the site of the old ferry at Clara Vale, with a young Basil Bunting at the left, and friends c.1907.

Basil Bunting at Brigflatts Friends Meeting House.

BASIL BUNTING
a northern life

Richard Caddel and Anthony Flowers

Newcastle Libraries & Information Service
in association with the Basil Bunting Poetry Centre, Durham

In memory of Tom Caddel
1976-1995

Thomas Lowe Bunting with Basil and Joyce, c.1910.

Contents

Acknowledgements

The authors would like to thank the following, without whose help this book would have been impossible to write—in particular the generous support of Basil Bunting's family: his widow Sima Bunting, his children Maria and Tom Bunting, and John Halliday as executor for the Estate. The invaluable assistance of Basil Bunting's nephew, Sandy Christie, is also gratefully acknowledged.

Neil Benson, Executive Editor, Newcastle Chronicle & Journal Ltd., for kindly granting permission to use quotations from old copies of company newspapers and reproduce photographs from their collection.

Carl Burn; Peter Daniels; Frederick A. Davies, Hon. Archivist, Ackworth School; Jimmy Donald; Dorothy Ellison; Tommy Hewitson; Dick Keys; Christopher Limb; Barry MacSweeney; Peter Makin; Frank Manders; Arthur Merrill; the Estate of Raymond Moore; Margaret Norwell; Tim R. Newell Price, Hon. Archivist, Leighton Park School; Peter Quartermain; Beth Rainey; Colin Simms; Derek Smith; Ian Swann; John Tones; Gael Turnbull; Desmond Walton; George Walton; Jack Wigham; Jonathan Williams; Bill Williamson; Violet Wilson; Malcolm Wright.

Quotations from Bunting's poems are reproduced with permission from Oxford University Press.

Material from the Basil Bunting Poetry Archive is reproduced with permission of Durham University Library.

All photographs unless otherwise acknowledged are in the possession of Alexander Christie © 1997.

The help given by the staff of the Basil Bunting Poetry Archive, Newcastle Libraries & Information Service, Tyne & Wear Archives, West Newcastle Local Studies, and the Library of Friends House has been invaluable.

Special thanks to Anna Flowers for her support during the research and writing of this book.

© Anthony Flowers and Richard Caddel, 1997.

Basil Bunting's poems © The Estate of Basil Bunting 1994.

ISBN: 1 85795 058 5

Cover photographs:

Basil Bunting beside the Rawthey, Cumbria 1980 © Jonathan Williams.

Basil Bunting seen against St Nicholas' Cathedral, Newcastle upon Tyne c.1965.

© Newcastle Chronicle & Journal Ltd.

Title page:

Basil Bunting from a studio portrait c.1916.

Cataloguing-in-publication data: a catalogue record for this book is available from the British Library.

City of Newcastle upon Tyne
Community & Leisure Services Department
Newcastle Libraries & Information Service, 1997.

Printed by Hindson Print Ltd., Newcastle upon Tyne.

Foreword

'A man's circumstances seldom matter to those who enjoy what he makes. We buy our shirts without asking who the seamstress was, and should read our poems without paying too much attention to the names they are printed over. Things once made stand free of their makers, the more anonymous the better. However, there are exceptions.'

Basil Bunting *The Selected Poems of Joseph Skipsey* 1976.

It is fairly certain that Basil Bunting would not have approved of this book. In a printed conversation with his friend the poet, Jonathan Williams he exclaimed: 'What the hell has any of this to do with the public? My autobiography is *Briggflatts*—there's nothing else worth speaking aloud.' But in spite of this appealing passion throughout his life and work he did constantly allude to the places and events of his life, directly or obliquely, in a wealth of poems, letters and published interviews.[1]

It seems to us that a book which attempts to unravel some of the facts about Bunting's life in the North and more particularly how his experience of the North helped to frame his ideas and ultimately his poems, would prove useful to all who are interested in either Bunting or the history and culture of the region.

When we began our research Bunting had been dead for nearly ten years and although much critical exegesis had been published, it seemed that few had sought to examine the details of what had been a complex life. Most had been content to rely without question on what Bunting himself had said. This book also makes much use of archival material to develop the biographical material that Bunting left us in interviews, including *Descant on Rawthey's Madrigal* and Sister Victoria Forde's *The Poetry of Basil Bunting*. Peter Makin's important study *Bunting: The Shaping of his Verse* has been drawn upon, as well as the various Oxford editions of his poems, and the publications of the Basil Bunting Poetry Centre in Durham. Yet even here in his native North East the man and his work remain largely unknown. It is time therefore to consider the man who has left us some of the most enduring poetry of the twentieth century, and trace his all-important relationship with his home place.

The Cheesman family in 1887, believed to have been taken at Hill House, Throckley.

Isaac Taylor Cheesman (Basil Bunting's grandfather) is standing at the rear with Nicholas, Lizzie and Pollie. Jennie is kneeling with her arm on Maggie's left shoulder beside the family spaniel; immediately to her left is Isaac's father; next to him is Annie (Basil Bunting's mother) and then Annie (Isaac's wife) and Matthew.

Introduction

Basil Bunting was born and died in the North East of England. Neglected by critics until the publication of his long poem *Briggflatts* in 1965, he is now recognised as a central figure of twentieth century poetry, linking the high modernism of the first part of the century with newer voices which have emerged since the 1960s. It is received wisdom in literary circles that someone described as a 'local poet' is, in some way, minor: interesting in a regional context, but unable to rise above the limitations of his or her immediate surroundings. Can Shakespeare, Pope or Donne, runs the argument, be thus confined to their homes? Of course not ... In this context, Bunting's eagerness to define himself within his regional context is still seen by many critics as a limiting factor, rendering him exotic to southern ears in the same way as 'The Likely Lads'—or perhaps he was working for the (as yet unformed) Northumbrian Tourist Board? (The Greek Tourist Board quotes Homer: was he too *merely* local?)

And yet our twentieth century experience suggests otherwise: as Bunting's fellow poet William Carlos Williams ('the poet of Paterson, New Jersey') wrote: 'the local is the only true universal, upon which all art builds.' Bunting's use of his home world not just in *Briggflatts* but throughout his work, forms a reference point for all that is valued, all that is worth saving. The folk songs which formed his earliest memories informed his approach to lyric poetry. The gruff Anglo Saxon brevity which survives in local speech informed his poetic language (even in translations of Persian and Latin poets), and the landscape and social and political environment provided a backdrop never far away in any part of his work. Far from limiting our understanding of Bunting's achievement, it is hard to overstate the importance of Tyneside and Northumbria as recurrent presences in his work.

These days there is little doubt of Bunting's worth—but readings of his work still suffer from dearly cherished myths about his life, many of which he started himself. One of the most prevalent myths is that he absented himself from his native Tyneside and Northumberland for about half a century: 'For the best part of fifty years Bunting did live virtually everywhere else but the North East', writes one author local enough to know better. We know that he lived a wandering life but how does this assertion of *'virtually everywhere else but'* stand up to examination?

In the 1900s and 1910s he lived mostly on Tyneside, apart from spells away at Quaker schools (Ackworth and Leighton Park) and formative visits to

Blucher miners c.1900. At this time Basil Bunting's grandfather, Isaac Taylor Cheesman, was manager of the Throckley Coal Company's Blucher Pit.

West Newcastle Local Studies

the Quaker hamlet of Brigflatts in Cumbria (still, according to Bunting's definition, in the old Northumbria).

In the 1920s and 1930s his wandering took him to London, America, France, Italy, the Canaries and so forth. At the same time, letters show him spending considerable time at the family homes in Jesmond and (after his father's death) Throckley, teaching in a workers' college to the west of Newcastle, studying for his mariner's ticket at Nellist's Nautical School on Tyneside, and living in a shepherd's house near the Simonsides.

In the 1940s, the war took him, like many other Tynesiders, far away for a considerable time, and afterwards he stayed in Persia, first as a diplomat and RAF Intelligence Officer, and then as a *Times* journalist. But even in this eventful decade we find him visiting his mother in Throckley at every opportunity, writing letters about war-torn Newcastle to his American friend the poet Louis Zukofsky.

From the 1950s to his death in 1985 he lived in Tyneside or Northumberland, apart from trips (largely following his 'discovery' in the mid-1960s) to America and Canada: in this period he 'affirmed' to his growing international audience his pride and pleasure in his lifetime's home region and 'acknowledged land'.

Far from living 'everywhere else but the North East', Bunting maintained his personal links with the region which were so important throughout his life, so that, as our opening quote suggests, friends and literary peers such as Pound and Yeats were left in no doubt as to his origins. To some extent this regionality was adversarial (as Peter Quartermain has shown in *Basil Bunting: Poet of the North*): he was an anti-Londoner in a way which many would still find extreme.

In this book the affirmation of the North East in which he was raised and to which he returned at key periods in his life is demonstrated in the most direct and documentary manner. To North Easterners it emphasises the extent to which his achievement is theirs, and to which his inheritance is that of the region. To those so unfortunate as to be unfamiliar with the North East it asserts the realities of locality and language upon which work of great spirit and beauty has been built.

The Roman Wall at Cawfields looking east, 1938.

Early Years

Basil Cheesman Bunting was born on 1 March 1900 at 27 Denton Road, Scotswood-on-Tyne. His father, Thomas Lowe Bunting, came from Heanor in Derbyshire and was an eminent doctor, with an extensive practice in the West End of Newcastle and was also the pit doctor for Montague Colliery, Scotswood-on-Tyne. His mother, Annie Cheesman, was the daughter of Isaac Taylor Cheesman who was manager and agent for W. Stephenson and Son's Old Throckley Colliery and manager for the Throckley Coal Company's Isabella, Derwentwater and Blucher Pits. It was the Cheesmans and their circle in Throckley who were to provide Basil Bunting with his strongest sense of locality and the northern mining tradition.

Basil Bunting aged about one year with his mother Annie.

Scotswood in 1900 was part of Benwell township. It was a relatively small community, essentially a colliery village for the Montague Colliery, surrounded by fields and growing industries along the banks of the Tyne to the west of Newcastle. Some of Bunting's earliest memories were of salmon being landed from the Tyne and loaded onto carts, of long walks across the fields of neighbouring farms to Newcastle, and of his Northumbrian nurse singing folksongs.

Dr Bunting was a well known and highly-esteemed member of the medical profession. He came to Scotswood in 1895 and lived at 17 Prospect Terrace, Scotswood-on-Tyne in that year, a small house in a terrace overlooking the River Tyne. Here he established his practice in a house which had been occupied by surgeons since 1892, and in 1899 he moved to 27 Denton Road. On 1 November 1898 he married Annie Cheesman at the parish church of St Michael and All Angels, Newburn. He had a brilliant university career taking his MD Degree (Gold Medal) at Edinburgh in 1904, his MB, CM degrees having been conferred in 1889. In an obituary he is described as being: 'keenly interested in the politico-social movements of the time, a man of rather advanced views who did not hesitate to express his opinions though these were never rigidly enforced, nor was he disagreeable in discussion. His patience and understanding and above all his grasp of complex issues was notable'. In conversation in 1968 Bunting remembered his father with affection: 'He was a doctor—a rather remarkable one. At that time [1903-4] he would still be busy preparing the thesis for his MD, which got him a Gold Medal at Edinburgh, in a tiny surgery with a desk about 2 feet by 18 inches and a microscope. He managed to compare the histology (histological structure, cell structure) of the lymphatic glands of very nearly all the mammals, and a good many other creatures too. There was in those days an animal shop in Newcastle and he had an arrangement when an animal died he would be called at once to go and remove the particular glands he wanted to examine before anything else was

done. So he managed to have lions, tigers, leopards, monkeys, all sorts of things on his list besides the small animals he could buy for the purpose. The house was sometimes full of lizards that had escaped from their box in the cellar.'[2]

The house in Denton Road was quite modest, (hence the tiny surgery, which was at the back of the house, reached by a dark passageway[3]) which makes Bunting's father's achievement all the more remarkable; the larger animals listed above are likely to have been obtained from one of the static circuses or travelling animal shows that were to be found in Newcastle's Haymarket at the time. Eventually Dr Bunting took up the study of radiology, visiting various important centres where X-ray work was being carried on, although his son tersely remarked: 'I think he spent more on machines than he ever got back from practice.' Nevertheless, he achieved considerable success in the practice of radiology, and when World War I broke out, he was provided with a unique opportunity to apply his skills.

left: Scotswood Bridge and Scotswood in 1910, seen from Derwenthaugh.

right: Junction of Fowberry Road and Denton Road c.1908. Number 27 lies just off centre, below the buildings of the Blaydon and District Industrial and Provident Society Limited. Thomas Lowe Bunting moved here in 1899 and it was still in use as his surgery when he died in 1925. Basil Bunting was born here in 1900.

In 1968 Bunting described his early schooling: 'I suppose about 1906 I did start school, I used to be taken by the housemaid. It was a long walk [from 27 Denton Road], about a mile and a half to the tram terminus, and then a considerable ride in the tram, and away up the hill to a part of Newcastle that is now all slums, which was then slightly shabby middle-class. There was an old lady who kept a school, a very old-fashioned kind.' This was Miss A.M. Bell's school at 24 West Parade, Rye Hill, a Dame's school of which there were a number at the time largely serving the middle classes. According to Bunting, Miss Bell: 'called it *kindergarten*, but I don't think she had the faintest notion what the word implied in the history of education. It was just a fashionable word. It was what you would call a day-nursery school in the old style.' Bunting and his sister Joyce also had a governess, a Miss Wraith. She was a kind young woman who loved her charges, but Bunting was to remember her frequent use of the cane. There are no traces of Bunting writing poetry at this early stage—indeed, his sister Joyce recalled that it was she, not Basil, who amused the family with comic verse in those days. After Miss Bell's school there seems some confusion as to his subsequent education.

In a *curriculum vitae* produced in 1952, Bunting writes that he attended the Royal Grammar School, Newcastle upon Tyne from 1909 to 1911. He was to repeat this claim later in life; however the school has no records to support this. Bunting's sister Joyce went for a while to Newcastle Central High School and subsequently to St Leonard's School at St Andrew's, on the east coast of Scotland.

Basil Bunting with his sister Joyce and their cousin Nancy Robson, pictured with the maids Anne and Polly. Thought to have been taken at the rear of 27 Denton Road, Scotswood c.1905.

Salmon fishermen under Scotswood Bridge, pre-World War I. This scene was commonplace in the nineteenth and early twentieth century and formed one of Basil Bunting's earliest memories. Gradually salmon catches declined as the Tyne became polluted by the sewage and industrial waste discharged directly into it, and commercial salmon-fishing became unviable. The salmon have now returned.

Ackworth and Leighton Park

Between 1912 and 1916 Bunting attended Ackworth School, a co-educational Quaker school near Pontefract in Yorkshire, and thereafter another Quaker school, Leighton Park in Berkshire, from 1916 to 1918. It is not known why Thomas Lowe Bunting decided to send his son to these particular schools. A surviving minute of the Ackworth Governing Body School Committee dated 26 March 1912 merely records: 'Application is made for the following non-members whose cases are decided as under, Basil Cheesman Bunting @ £54 p.a.' This was the standard boarding fee for the time. Five other pupils were admitted at the same time. This period was one of rising prosperity for the family; Bunting's father had developed a very successful practice in the West End of Newcastle and while Bunting was away at school the family moved to 38 Moorside, Fenham, a developing middle-class suburb of Newcastle.

Bunting was happy at Ackworth, which provided a very broad and liberal education. Pupils grew the vegetables that they ate and milked cows and all students attended regular Bible classes. Bunting made firm friends with two boys who started on the same day, 12 September 1912. His most cherished friend was Ernest Cooper Apperley Stephenson, the son of Ernest and Edith Stephenson of Yeardon near Leeds. Stephenson was nearly two years older than Bunting, and he developed an enduring affection for his school friend. In the last years of his life Bunting planned to write about Stephenson as an act of remembrance—but this act remained unfinished at his death.

In 1913—at the age of thirteen—Bunting visited Brigflatts the small Cumbrian Quaker hamlet for the first time, on the invitation of his other principal Ackworth school friend, John Allen Greenbank. Greenbank was the son of John Greenbank, a monumental mason, of High Brigflatts. John Allen Greenbank's sister Peggy was to become the dedicatee of one of Bunting's best early odes, Ode 1:3 *I am agog for foam* and *Briggflatts*. During this visit and on subsequent visits, Bunting began to attend meetings in the seventeenth-century Meeting House there. Though Bunting was profoundly affected by his Quaker education he stopped short of becoming a member of the Society of Friends, never describing himself as more than an *attender*; there are no records of his attending meetings in Newcastle.

In 1915 Bunting delivered a prize-winning paper on Walt Whitman, which is said to have won the attention of Edward Carpenter, the writer and socialist reformer and friend and advocate of Whitman's poetry. The Headmaster, Frederick Andrews commented on Bunting's essay at the end of term gathering on 30 June 1915: 'Basil Bunting with youthful ardour and perhaps more

Jesmond Road looking East c.1930. The Bunting family moved to Jesmond Road towards the end of World War I and were to remain in Jesmond until Thomas Lowe Bunting died in 1925.

than youthful erudition championed the poetry of Walt Whitman.' A month later Bunting was to satisfy the examiners in the Northern Universities school certificate examination. Bunting published two poems in 1916. 'The Song of the Ackworth Clock (by Basil C. Bunting leaver July 1916)' appeared in the Annual Report of the Headmaster of Ackworth School for 1916. It is hard to identify the progressive tastes of the writer on Whitman, with authorship of this extremely conventional school poem. In the summer of 1916 Bunting together with his friend Stephenson obtained the Senior School Certificate (Matriculation), with Distinction in English.

On 13 April 1916 Bunting's much loved Grandfather, Isaac Taylor Cheesman died, and was buried in St Michael and all Angels Church, Newburn. His death was keenly felt by the boy. Some months later, Thomas Lowe Bunting took the decision to move Bunting from Ackworth to Leighton Park, probably in order to give his son a greater chance of gaining entrance into Cambridge. Bunting's two friends left Ackworth at the same time: Greenbank to join the Friends Ambulance Unit, in which he served for the rest of the war; Stephenson to enlist in the armed forces.

In December 1916 Bunting had another poem published in *The Leightonian*, entitled *Keep Troth*. In the context of a stormy school career since his arrival at Leighton Park in September of that year it may seem a surprising poem. He had repeatedly expressed his unhappiness at the school, and in October he laid a remarkable document before Charles Evans, his headmaster: 'I have utterly failed to be happy here … I think there must be some great underlying difference between North & South which makes people with Northern manners comfortable & easy to deal with, but people with Southern manners are, for me, utterly "impossible" & hateful … I think it is your duty to give me my fare to Newcastle …' It is worth noting here that despite Bunting's obvious militant 'northern proclivities' on entry to Leighton Park, he had come from a northern school where in fact 36 per cent of the pupils were from the south of England.

Keep Troth, in which Quaker reliance upon inner truth triumphs over worldly conflict, may have its origins in the stern-but-fair talking-to which headmaster Evans gave him on this occasion. Bunting eventually came to terms with 'Southern manners', and seems to have had two solid years busying himself with things that interested him: he was to present papers on William Blake and Kerensky (the Russian democratic socialist who was successively minister of justice, minister of war and prime minister between the two revolutions of 1917)—with little hint of the turmoil that was to come.

Portland Terrace c.1930. The Buntings lived in a house to the right of this picture overlooking Portland Park, a pleasant outlook. The site of the park is now a bus depot, and the Buntings' house is occupied by bus company offices.

BRIGFLATTS FRIENDS' MEETING HOUSE BUILT 1675   Q.2.

Brigflatts Friends Meeting House taken from an old postcard. In 1975 Basil Bunting dedicated a late Ode to this place in which he had found peace and silence early and late in his life.

A rare snapshot photograph of Basil Bunting with his father Thomas Lowe Bunting, taken in 1916.

His final year at Leighton Park was concerned with matriculation for Cambridge. A letter from H.J. Edwards of Peterhouse, Cambridge, gives us an insight into the mind of the seventeen-year-old Bunting: 'The examiners reported that his work in Ancient History and Medieval European History was very promising, as regards both style and matter. In the paper of General Questions there were signs of immaturity and of a certain recklessness; and his English essay made a very unfavourable impression for its lack of taste and even of sense. His French was fair: in Latin he only just qualified.

It was felt that there was a possibility of brilliance in him, but that his work was as yet too uneven and unbalanced to merit the award of a Scholarship.'

However Bunting was to surmount his lamentable 'lack of taste' in literature, these comments are telling in that they identify the passion for history which was to remain with him throughout his life, remembered by friends and family alike—a passion which informed so much of his poetry.

The Ackworth School Leavers of 1916. Basil Bunting, John Allen Greenbank and Ernest Cooper Apperley Stephenson can be identified from the key on the right.

His Headmaster, Frederick Andrews BA, in a letter to Leighton Park, dated 30 May 1916, was to comment : 'I think Bunting does show real talent in literature and in grasp of history. I think his failure in Latin arises from a disinclination for its study—in past time he has worked at subjects he likes and given the go-bye to others— and now he finds it hard to recover lost ground. He is now much more amenable to advice and discipline—and will I think fall in comfortably with your school life.'

	Sixth Form, Boys & Girls. 6th June 1916.				
1	John Allen Greenbank.	7	Basil Cheesman Bunting.	13	MARY FORREST HARTLEY. B.A.
2	Alfred Dewhirst.	8	Ralph Edward Crockatt.	14	Maxwell Herbert Wray.
3	Kathleen Francis Benington.	9	Constane Winifred Butler.	15	John Clapham Knowles.
4	Ralph Dimmock Cass.	10	FREDERICK ANDREWS, B.A; J.P.	16	Stanley Smith.
5	Mira Marjorie Vardon.	11	Eileen Mary Little.	17	Maurice Daniel Sibson.
6	Thomas Gilbert Haslam.	12	Ernest Cooper Apperley Stephenson.	18	Ashton Watts.

The Objector

On 16 March 1918, shortly after his eighteenth birthday Bunting took his stand as a conscientious objector. He appeared for preliminary examination by the Military Service Representative at 26 Northumberland Street, Newcastle upon Tyne. On stating that he was not prepared to accept military service he was referred to the Newcastle Military Tribunal.

While awaiting his Tribunal in Newcastle, he received the news that his Ackworth friend Cooper Stephenson, by then a 2nd Lieutenant in the Royal Flying Corps, had been killed in action, on 21 March 1918.

Bunting's Tribunal took place a month later at the Town Hall on Wednesday 17 April 1918. He is described in a report in the *Newcastle Daily Journal*: 'A youth, 18 years of age, applied for exemption from military service. He had been educated at Quaker schools and in consequence he had imbibed a good deal of Quaker doctrine including their well known attitude to war.' The Tribunal offered him non-combatant service (a term that does not accurately describe the harsh reality), which he declined indicating that he would appeal against the decision.

Other newspapers of the time described the event of his Tribunal in more detail: the *North Mail* under the heading **OBJECTOR AT EIGHTEEN Newcastle Youth to Join Non-Combatant Corps**, is worth quoting at length:

> 'A conscientious objector to military service, who had reached in March last the mature age of 18 years, came before the Newcastle Tribunal yesterday. In a long statement the lad, who carried himself with great self-possession, objected to war, to non-combatant service because it released a man for combatancy, to national service because it helped the prosecution of war, and to leaving his present occupation of "desultory reading" because he thought he was doing his duty as a "citizen of the world" in remaining as he was. He had been educated in Quaker schools.
>
> In reply to Mr George Renwick, the applicant was quite prepared to let the German hordes overrun England.
>
> "Are you taught those principles in these Quaker schools?" asked Mr Renwick. "The whole atmosphere is one of pacifism," came the reply.
>
> Further replies of an equally uncompromising character led Mr Renwick sarcastically to observe: "You would rather stay here and let other men die for you in France?"
>
> "Yes," interposed the objector.
>
> "You are a beauty, you are!" said Mr Renwick.
>
> On hearing that the tribunal would grant him non-combatant service, the applicant inquired about appealing, whereat Mr Renwick indignantly broke in: "I want it to be clearly understood that I absolutely object to that—a boy of 18 coming here with such views."'

The *Illustrated Chronicle* published on the same day, Thursday 18 April, headed their report **NEWCASTLE 'CONCHY' Would sooner see Huns Over-running Country Than Kill a Man.**

OBJECTOR AT EIGHTEEN.

Newcastle Youth to Join Non-Combatant Corps.

A conscientious objector to military service, who had reached in March last the mature age of 18 years, came before the Newcastle Tribunal yesterday.

In a long statement the lad, who carried himself with great self-possession, objected to war, to non-combatant service because it released a man for combatancy, to national service because it helped the prosecution of war, and to leaving his present occupation of "desultory reading" because he thought he was doing his duty as a "citizen of the world" in remaining as he was. He had been educated in Quaker schools.

In reply to Mr George Renwick, the applicant was quite prepared to let the German hordes overrun England.

"Are you taught those principles in these Quaker schools?" asked Mr Renwick.

"The whole atmosphere is one of pacifism," came the reply.

Further replies of an equally uncompromising character led Mr Renwick sarcastically to observe: "You would rather stay here and let other men die for you in France?"

"Yes," interposed the objector.

"You are a beauty, you are!" said Mr Renwick.

On hearing that the tribunal would grant him non-combatant service, the applicant inquired about appealing, whereat Mr Renwick indignantly broke in: "I want it to be clearly understood that I absolutely object to that—a boy of 18 coming here with such views."

From the *North Mail*, Thursday, 18 April, 1918.

The Old Town Hall c.1915.
Basil Bunting's Tribunal took
place here in 1918.

'An 18-year-old youth applied at Newcastle Local Tribunal yesterday for exemption on conscientious grounds. He stated that he was a student of History, and had because of his views, sacrificed a scholarship at Peterhead [sic]. He had been educated at a Quaker school, where the whole atmosphere was one of pacifism. He had a conscientious objection to killing a man; it was manifestly wicked to do so after months of preparation. He could not take up non-combatant service because that meant releasing a man to do what he himself objected to do. By continuing his studies he considered he was doing what was best in the interest of the country. He would sooner see Germans over-running this country than kill a man.' The *Newcastle Weekly Chronicle*, reporting on Saturday 20 April 1918, took up the story in a similar vein under the heading:

A 'Conchy's' Appeal.

Evidently local newspapers covered the story with differing degrees of detail and opprobrium: these were the days when the popular press strongly supported the war effort, commemorating the recent dead with passport-sized photographs in a prominent back-page feature.

The Newcastle Panel of the Northumberland Appeal Tribunal sat at the Education Offices, Newcastle upon Tyne on Thursday 20 June 1918. and Bunting appeared before the local historian F.W. Dendy. The *Newcastle Daily Journal* on 21 June commented thus: 'An eighteen year old conscientious objector, a history student, appearing for exemption. He was given a month to take up agricultural work or join up. He said he did not think he could accept the condition.'

Bunting could not be supported in his position by his family. His father was prominent in Newcastle medical life and had been radiologist at the Northumberland War Hospital in Gosforth since the Autumn of 1914. Housed in St Nicholas' Hospital, the city's lunatic asylum, its former patients having been moved out for the duration of the war, this hospital was dealing with so many war wounded that a special railway line had to be constructed to allow troop trains of wounded to disembark at the main entrance, direct from the South. Many thousands of casualties were treated here during the course of the war.

Bunting's subsequent time as a conscientious objector led to a reticence about the experience that was to remain with him, and was to mark a turning point in his life. Without doubt he would have

Northumberland War Hospital, Gosforth.

The Northumberland War Hospital in Gosforth taken from an old postcard.

been subject to harsh treatment, although the confinement of conscientious objectors in public civil prisons rather than in the hands of the Army, had eased the situation. The case of the Richmond Sixteen (a well documented case involving murderous treatment meted out to sixteen northern conscientious objectors held for some time in Richmond Castle) showed the extreme lengths that the Army was prepared to go to in its treatment of those who refused to fight. It is worth considering that during World War I seventy-four conscientious objectors died as a result of mistreatment by the Army.

At first Bunting was held in the Guardroom at Fenham Barracks. In conversation with Peter Quartermain in 1984 he described the conditions there: ' ... a large, crowded, unheated 18th-century-style room. The police and the army always picked up all male prisoners on release or even on bail to see if they wanted them for the army ... his companions were mainly pickpockets and thieves. It was cold, most prisoners were grown men, not boys of 18. A few blankets were provided over which the prisoners fought. One prisoner a large and angry man, managed to get two blankets, one of which he gave to Bunting. He was the only person in that room to treat him with kindness ... he was talkative, pleasant and kind ... and remanded for a double murder, poisoning two women'.

Some background on conscription in the North East is perhaps helpful. Voluntary enlistment which had been organised by Lord Derby, the then Secretary of State for War, in October 1914 was to prove inadequate in providing sufficient manpower for the replacement and reinforcement of the British forces in France. By January 1916 Military Conscription was introduced for single men, and by May 1916 it was extended to include married men between the ages of eighteen and forty-one. The Military Service Acts gave statutory authority to local tribunals to examine cases for exemption from military service. There were four grounds for exemption: economic distress to one's self and dependents; reserved occupations; physical ill-health and conscientious objection. Local Tribunals manned by local councillors and businessmen were able to grant either absolute, temporary or conditional exemption or dismiss the application.

THE MEDICAL STAFF.

The Medical staff of The Northumberland War Hospital. Thomas Lowe Bunting is in the centre to the rear of the group.

In March 1916 there were about 2,000 Local Tribunals which were part of the Government's scheme to implement the 'total war effort'. By 1917 casualties were so great that Tribunals were pressured to provide their respective 'county quota' of men for the front and in May of that year it was said by the Secretary of State for War that: 'I don't hesitate to say that 80 per cent of the ordinary Tribunals of the Country, are failing in their work at the present moment.'

On Wednesday 10 April 1918 Lloyd George was to be reported in the *Newcastle Daily Journal* as stating to the house: 'There was an understanding as to boys under 19 years of age that they were only to be used in case of emergency. We felt the emergency had arisen, and those over 18 and a half who had received six months training we felt it necessary to send as drafts.' In such a context it was inevitable that Bunting's case would be received with little sympathy.

What happened to Bunting subsequent to the Tribunal and his Appeal remains unclear, as official records from this time appear to be missing. After the month was up he is likely to have been arrested and handed over to the Military Authorities. The Northumberland Fusiliers would have kept him at the Barracks for a period of a month, he would then be asked to put on a uniform, and he would refuse. He would then be put on 'jankers' (military prison work as a punishment for defaulters) for another month when he would be asked to put on the uniform again. After this refusal he would have been handed over to the civil authorities. It was government policy, in order to minimise mistreatment, to place conscientious objectors in civil prisons usually away from where they lived, or where there were cells available. They were made to wear special uniforms that distinguished them from other prisoners. It is therefore not surprising to find that Bunting was subsequently imprisoned out of the North. His old school magazine *The Leightonian* for December 1918 states that 'B.C. Bunting is serving a sentence of 112 days in Wormwood Scrubs, after refusing agricultural work on the ground that in effect that was sending another man to fight for him.' The July 1919 edition prints part of a letter from Bunting: 'I am able to answer your letter myself, because it arrived here just two or three days after I was released under the Cat and Mouse Act. I spent all last autumn and winter in Wormwood Scrubs Prison, making mailbags and twisting ships' fenders [rope buffers to protect the sides of a ships]. I forfeited my remission, because for some while before the armistice I refused to do

prison work, so I was not released until the end of January. Then I had divers adventures, into which I need not now enter, and after a long sojourn in a military hospital, whither I was sent to get rid of a septic ulcer, I found myself on Salisbury Plain. There after I had visited Stonehenge, and satisfied myself as to the internal appearance of Y.M.C.A. huts, I repeated the farce of refusing to obey an order, for which I was court-martialled a second time, and sent to do a year's hard labour in Winchester Civil Prison. There were only half a dozen C.O.s left there, all the rest having been released under the twenty months order, and since I did not see why the rest of us should be left behind, I went on hunger strike. They were very merciful with me. I have come to the conclusion that they only wanted an excuse to let me out, because three days proved sufficient to do the trick, and they gave me six weeks (till June 15th) to do as I like in.'

On June 24th 1919 Bunting visited Leighton Park in person and informed them cheerfully that he was living in London and avoiding the police. He was on the threshold of adulthood, and about to embark on his literary career.

above left: 'Feed the Guns Week', Newcastle upon Tyne 1918. Basil Bunting is thought to have been in prison during this fund-raising week.

left: Recruiting Poster, Newcastle upon Tyne c.1916.

above right: Newcastle Barracks, Barrack Road, Fenham, c.1910. Basil Bunting was imprisoned in the Guardroom here in 1918, subsequent to his removal to Wormwood Scrubs Prison.

right: A much later view in the 1960s after the Barracks had been demolished. Basil Bunting was held in the guardroom to the left of the main gate, which is in the centre of this photograph. It is easily identified from the plan and matches Bunting's description of the room.

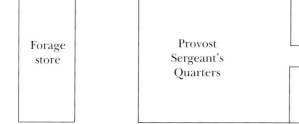
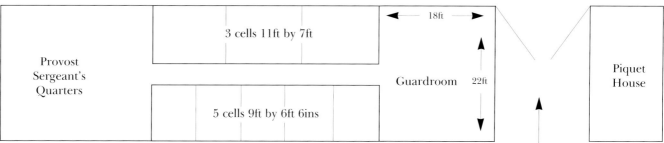

Forage store	Provost Sergeant's Quarters	

3 cells 11ft by 7ft

18ft

Guardroom 22ft

5 cells 9ft by 6ft 6ins

Piquet House

A plan of the guardroom and cells, pre-1914.

Main Barracks RA entrance

only bricks and bleak black cement and bricks,
only the military tread and the snap of the locks.
    Mine was a threeplank bed whereon
I lay and cursed the weary sun.
They took away the prison clothes
and on the frosty nights I froze.
I had a Bible where I read
that Jesus came to raise the dead—
I kept myself from going mad
by singing an old bawdy ballad
and birds sang on my windowsill
and tortured me till I was ill, ...

from *Villon*, 1925

c.1920 Basil Bunting with his cousin Basil Cheesman and
Jack the dog, taken in Northumberland after his release
from prison.

Leaving Home

In *The Leightonian* for July 1920 Bunting is said to be: 'still at the London School of Economics. He is hoping to go to Russia shortly via Copenhagen, but the Danish authorities say that the "desire to study Danish Literature is not a good enough lie and refuse to *viser* his passport." Meanwhile he has been appointed to write articles on English art, music and literature, for a Roumanian newspaper. He is also growing a beard.'

He had thrown himself into Bohemian literary London. 'Poet appointed' he later wrote in *Briggflatts* 'dare not decline / to walk among the bogus'. The next two decades were to be the most 'wandering' period of his life—the period when he came into contact with the great modernist writers (Ford Madox Ford, Ernest Hemingway, T.S. Eliot, Mina Loy, Ezra Pound, James Joyce, W.B. Yeats and others) and he developed in confidence as a poet. But even in this period, north-eastern contacts and associates were to play their part.

Bunting's family had moved house again, as his father's career advanced: just before the outbreak of war, while still retaining his practice in Scotswood, Dr Bunting had obtained a position as Physician to the Electrical Department at the Fleming Memorial Hospital for Sick Children at Moor Edge in Jesmond. Some time in 1918 they moved briefly to 95 Jesmond Road, then a short distance away to a substantial house with a pleasant outlook at 6 Portland Terrace. Conditions in Portland Terrace were somewhat cramped as the house was shared with Thomas Lowe's sister, Sarah Anna. They were to remain here until Bunting's father died in 1925.

Contacts with Newcastle cultural life continued to be important and formative: a close neighbour at this time was the Newcastle-born composer and musicologist William Gillies Whittaker who lived nearby in Jesmond at 4 Granville Road. Whittaker was an important collector and editor of Northumbrian folk songs, giving lectures on the subject at Newcastle Literary and Philosophical Society during this period and writing informative articles on it, in a tone which Bunting was to echo in much of his own music journalism. Bunting attended rehearsals of Whittaker's Newcastle Bach Choir, and was present at the memorable first performance of Byrd's *Great Service* given by the choir in Newcastle Cathedral on 31 May 1924. This important work was being performed for the first time in its entirety since the time of William Byrd (1543-1623), having recently been re-edited from parts discovered in Durham Cathedral, by Dr Fellowes. Remarkably for the time, the *Magnificat* and the *Nunc Dimittis* were relayed live from the Cathedral by the local Newcastle radio station. Bunting's Aunt Jennie Cheesman (Mrs Tom Lamb) was a long standing member of the Newcastle and Gateshead Choral Union under Whittaker, and as a member of the Newcastle Bach Choir sang in this and subsequent performances of the *Great Service*. Whittaker's influence on the young Bunting was to extend to that of musical performance: Bunting owned a copy of Whittaker's *North Countrie Ballads, Songs and Pipe-tunes*, from which he played (on recorders) and sang throughout his life.

The family's socialist sympathies are significant. On arriving in Newcastle in 1898, Thomas Lowe Bunting joined the old Fabian Society, at that time the nursery of George Bernard Shaw, Sidney Webb and Graham Wallas and other influential thinkers. After the First World War Bunting was to

Thomas Lowe Bunting and Jack the dog, possibly taken at the rear of 6 Portland Terrace.

contribute footnotes to the Prison System Enquiry Committee of the Labour Research Department, whose report, *English Prisons Today*, caused a sensation and led to the Royal Commission on Prison Reform. In later life Bunting described Wallas as an inspired lecturer, who could make any subject interesting, with students at the London School of Economics fighting to get into his lectures. Bunting himself became a Fabian around the age of sixteen. During these early years in London, Bunting recalled having tea and toast in the Fabian common room above its shop in Westminster in 1919, where he met most of the eminent Fabians of the time. Bunting's father also provided him with early contact with Newcastle's cultural and literary life. In 1898 Thomas Lowe Bunting had joined the Literary and Philosophical Society in Westgate Road. The Lit and Phil acted as a focus for ideas and thinkers in the area, and had a renowned library and a wide-ranging lecture programme. Bunting's father was to be associated with the Lit and Phil until he died in 1925, and his mother and aunt Sarah Anna were also members. Bunting himself was elected in 1968 becoming an Honorary member in 1978.

It is worth noting that Ezra Pound, the poet who perhaps more than any other influenced Bunting, and championed his work, visited the Lit and Phil on Monday 3 November 1919. He gave a lecture on the Troubadours with illustrations, (presumably recited or sung) to an audience of 714 people. The capacity of the lecture theatre at the Lit and Phil at this time was around 850, so this figure represents a sizeable audience for what must have been a fairly esoteric subject, but unfortunately it seems that Pound's lecture does not survive. In the light of Pound's subsequent importance to Bunting it is tempting to speculate that he, along with his father or other members of his family, was present in the audience.

At about the same time, or soon afterwards, Bunting was entering the London literary circle of Nina Hamnett. She gave him a copy of Pound's *Homage to Sextus Propertius*, perhaps the most important step in Bunting's development as a poet.

Bunting spent a short period at the London School of Economics, specialising in currency, but left in 1921 without taking a degree, which he was later to ascribe to his inability to do statistics. He briefly became secretary for Harry Barnes, a Newcastle architect and Coalition Liberal MP for East Newcastle. Barnes, from September 1916 to March 1918, had been County Adjutant of the Northumberland Volunteer Force, and from March 1918 Commanding Officer of the 2nd Volunteer Battalion Northumberland Fusiliers with the rank of Major. In hindsight we can see the irony of the situation of his employing a recently released conscientious objector. In a 1969 interview Bunting was to describe the experience dryly: 'I was young then and I imagined that members of Parliament were serious people. That must have been one of the worst parliaments of all time. Six hundred black-hearted villains. Not that I think that things have improved much.'

In his early twenties he began to support himself with occasional journalism. His wanderings began in earnest in 1923 when he was in Paris where he dug roads, worked as an artists' model and became assistant editor for the writer Ford Madox Ford on *the transatlantic review*: 'I got tired of living with Ford. However much you liked and admired him it was an impossible situation for a young man. He lived in a state of perpetual hysteria. He'd bury his great ugly head on your shoulder and weep. It was too much responsibility for a young person, so I cleared out. I'd saved £20, and with that I went to Italy. I loved Italy. If you could cut yourself off from where you belong—which you can't—I'd find it hard to choose between Italy and Persia.'

He returned to England in December 1923, gave up his position on *the transatlantic review*, and in early 1924 arrived in Italy, in Rapallo—near his mentor Ezra Pound, who was then resident there.

In 1924 Dr Bunting became seriously ill with angina and was in great pain. Bunting returned home and sought work locally, complaining to his friends of the problems involved, until his father died on 25 February 1925 and was buried in Jesmond Old Cemetery near Portland Terrace (as his wife and sister were to be in their turn). Thomas Lowe Bunting's will was proved on 30 March 1925. It did not mention Bunting or his sister Joyce, but named his father's sisters, Sarah Anna (who received £600), and Harriet Alice (£300); the Legal Executrix and residuary legatee was Annie Bunting.

Newburn Road, Newburn. 8131

Newburn Road, Throckley 1930. Annie Bunting was to move here to number 242—known locally as the Villas—after the death of Thomas Lowe Bunting in 1925. Basil Bunting was to regard this house as his home until he moved to Shadingfield, Wylam in 1957.

After the comfortable existence as the wife of a successful doctor, Annie Bunting and her children found that they were no longer well off. She was unable to retain the house in Jesmond, and moved to Throckley, close to other members of the Cheesman family. Bunting remembered this house as being more spacious, presumably because his aunt no longer lived with them.

In a letter to his London friend, the poet J.J. Adams (19 February 1926), he described life in the winter of 1926 as 'the hardest of winters, and so very poor indeed, and mother used to affluence.' In the same letter he describes how he attempted to support himself and his mother: 'I became one of the ignoble army of lecturers who pretends to educate adults. I lecture on economics to workingmen, confuse their minds with the technicalities of the money market, and get two pounds a week for it.' He went on to describe where he lectured on currency and anthropology as 'a workingmen's college at Lemington Settlement', near where he was

Newcastle Chronicle & Journal Ltd.

The pit head scene after the Montague Colliery disaster on 30 March 1925. This pit disaster was strikingly similar to that described by Basil Bunting in *They Say Etna*.

living in Throckley. This was in fact the Adult School in Montague Street, Lemington. It had been founded in 1913 by Dr Andrew Messer,[5] Bunting's uncle, who lived nearby in Union Hall Road, Lemington. During 1926 WEA classes proliferated providing striking miners and unemployed workmen with time on their hands an opportunity to discuss contemporary issues in comfortable surroundings. Bunting was also ghost-writing speeches and lectures for Lord Kirkley and others.

Here, his associations with the region's mining concerns were of course to the fore: in a later letter to Ezra Pound (21 March 1934) he wrote of this time: 'I was on the spot when the View Pit was flooded and forty-five men drowned, I heard what the men had to say about it and the whole cursed system when there wasn't any question of politics mining or otherwise, but just sheer human commonsense. My Grandfather, whom I knew pretty well when I was a kid, was a miner, son of a miner. I know the solidity of these people, and I watched it break up in 26, when I was all the time in a mining village, took the chair at one of Cook's[6] meetings, stuck a knife in the tyres of of a government strikebreaking lorry and tried unsuccessfully nearly every paper in the country to get the scandalous faked benches of magistrates who condemned the strikers to years of hard labour shown up. Not even the independent labour party's rag would publish the facts.' In an uncollected poem written for Ezra Pound, *They say Etna*, Bunting was to visit this territory again:

Gear, then, and gear,
                gritty grinding.
The governor spins, raises its arms.
Two three-inch steel cables scream from the drum
seventy fathoms.
We carry lighted Davy lamps,
stoop along narrow track.
Trucks scold tunnel.
In a squat cavern a
naked man on his
knees with a
pickaxe rips a nugget from the coalface.

Four lads
        led the pownies
a mile and a half through rising water,
lampless because the stife
asphyxiates lamps,
by old galleries to the North Shaft.
The water rose.
                The others
came five months later when it was pumped out
and were buried by public subscription.
(The widows were provided for.)

Two pit boys who were rescued.

From *Newcastle Daily Chronicle* 31 March 1925.

This closely matches accounts of the disaster at View Pit, or 'Low Monty', on 30 March 1925, when miners broke through into the disused workings of the neighbouring Paradise Pit in Benwell. Millions of gallons of water flooded in and thirty-eight men and boys died either through drowning or were asphyxiated by 'black damp'. The curious spelling of *pownies* is interesting: this is a direct transliteration of the local Throckley dialect, which pronounced the word pony, 'powny'. The local Throckley dialect has been well documented: Bill Williamson in *Class, Culture And Community* describes the language of his grandfather, a miner who lived in Throckley, as being a soft Northumbrian accent with rolling 'r's, liberally sprinkled with the archaic pronouns 'thee' and 'thou'. Bunting's much-loved grandfather Isaac Taylor Cheesman and his uncle Matthew Taylor Cheesman (both Throckley men) would have used this dialect, and Bunting would have grown up used to hearing it being spoken. Bunting's own speech—both in poetry reading and in conversation—had much of this local quality.

Bywell 1936, with the two churches St Andrew and St Peter. Basil Bunting was to list Bywell as one of the most important places in the region, and included it in one of his early poems:

I thought I saw my late wife (a very respectable woman)
coming from Bywell churchyard with a handful of raisins.
I was not pleased, it is shocking to meet a ghost, so I cut her
and went and sat amongst the rank watergrasses by the Tyne.

Attis: or, something missing, 1931

Rothbury c.1930 seen from Bilberry Hill. When at Coldside Bunting's walk to Rothbury used to bring him to the top of Simonside. 'It was a very pleasant place up there. I learned a little about how they train sheepdogs'.

The accent which Bunting carried with him all his life is thus evidently the highly specific, local language from the place where, and the people amongst whom, he spent his childhood. Listening to recordings of him today, 'southrons' unaware of this context have pronounced his accent 'affected': with local knowledge we can see that Bunting got his specific poetic language—like much of his culture, music and politics—from the particular area in which he grew up.

In 1928 Bunting was coming to his wits' end, from a spell as a hack journalist for a number of London weeklies (he claimed to have written both Labour and Tory leaders) when he received some financial help from an American benefactor in his London literary circle, Margaret de Silver. This period of short-lived financial security enabled him to spend some time in the Simonside hills in Northumberland. In 1930, in his first 'slim volume' of poetry (privately published in Milan) he was to write of this period: 'I thank Margaret de Silver for bailing me out of Fleet Street; after two years convalescence from an attack of journalism I am beginning to recover my honesty.'

He stayed with Edward 'Ned' Wilson, (a shepherd for tenant farmer 'Matty' Milburn of Lordenshaws), who was then living at Coldside Farm, Forestburn Gate in the Simonside hills near Rothbury. Wilson (not the sheepdog trainer Wilson of *Briggflatts*) normally shepherded at Spylaw, high and isolated in the hills, but was unwell with a stomach complaint that made it difficult for him to work, although he helped with lambing and haymaking, which necessitated the move to Coldside Farm. To make ends meet his wife took in paying guests. Wilson's daughter, who was six at the time, remembers Bunting with his moustache and pipe—not surprisingly she found him intimidating! He was writing during the time he was staying with them, and she was under strict instructions not to disturb him.

Bunting appears to have been living at Coldside during the autumn of 1928. Throughout 1928 he wrote a monthly music column, 'Music of the Month', for *The Town Crier* (a cultural monthly which published articles on craft, clothing, architecture and gardening as well as reviews, recipes and so on). Bunting's first entry (in the December issue for 1927) was prefaced with this introduction: 'Those of our readers who have been asking us for so long to include musical articles among the features of *The Town Crier* will be glad to hear that we have been able to secure the services of Mr. Basil Bunting, who

© Anthony Flowers

Coldside from a photograph taken in 1996, with Simonside in the background. Spylaw lies high up the fell just off centre.

(Lower left) Ned and Violet Wilson and Matty Milburn with sheepdogs, seen at Coldside in 1928.

will write us regular articles on music of the month.'

In the September 1928 issue of *The Town Crier*, Bunting is clearly away from London and relishing his Northumbria, as he writes: 'This is the close season for music. Theosophists and Spiritualists possess the halls. The virtuosi are on holiday or turning up at short notice to play unrehearsed concertos at the Proms ... The critic, who has stoically endured for a whole year every kind of organised noise that man can hope to get his fellow man to pay for, has now suddenly found that the sounds that are supplied to Londoners gratis—to wit, motor-horns, accelerating 'buses, back-firing exhausts, drays, newsboys, street-organs and drunks, all restlessly modulating on a pedal-point of rubber-on-asphalt—are more than a mind with the acquired habit of listening can put up with for more than two years in succession without a break. There is a tale of a pianist who, having played a repeat passage as far as the double bars twice, forgot the bridge passage that followed and had to go on repeating and repeating until at last he broke down from sheer fatigue. London is such a pianist rendered tireless. The Traffic Symphony is not unstimulating to a country hearer; but after the seven hundredth and thirtieth repetition one prays for a transport workers' strike, a long one, or to become temporarily deaf. Therefore this is written from the country, where there is not silence, but a change of noise, a piano for a forte and an andante for a presto.' The 'Traffic Symphony' stayed with him, and was recalled years later in *Briggflatts*: the London poet writes:

© Violet Wilson

> counts beat against beat, bus conductor
> against engine against wheels against
> the pedal, Tottenham Court Road, decodes
> thunder ...

But the Northumbrian life and landscape made a far deeper impression upon him.

In a letter to Leippert (30 October 1932) he wrote: 'I was for some years in England, earning a very meagre living and growing stupid. Then I kicked, decided that I'd rather not earn a living than write any more reviews for weeklies, and have been better for it ever since. I tried my own North Country for a while, and it wasn't so bad but I got very little done that I wanted to keep, so I took advice and went to Berlin and it was the worst thing I ever did.'

He may have 'got very little done' in his period in Northumberland, but what he did was of lasting interest, particularly since it presages concerns which were to return to him later in life. In two odes, *Gin the Goodwife Stint* and *The Complaint of the Morpethshire Farmer* he draws on local shepherds' experiences of land clearance and forced emigration which was prevalent in the area at that time: here is *Gin the Goodwife Stint*, an ode dated 1930:

> The ploughland has gone to bent
> and the pasture to heather;
> gin the goodwife stint,
> she'll keep the house together.
>
> Gin the goodwife stint
> and the bairns hunger
> the Duke can get his rent
> one year longer.
>
> The Duke can get his rent
> and we can get our ticket
> twa pund emigrant
> on a C.P.R. packet.

A CPR packet was an emigration ship of the Canadian Pacific Railways, offering one-way tickets to Canada at £2, and The 'Duke' was 'Matty' Milburn's landlord, the Duke of Northumberland who came in for more stick in *They say Etna*, where he appears as the Duke of Slumberland.

Bunting's favourite Aunt Jennie—the singer in Byrd's *Great Service*—had emigrated to Canada with her farmer husband Tom in 1926, and so we can imagine that Bunting felt deeply and was well informed about rural clearances in Northumberland at this time.

Ezra Pound was a supporter of this group of Bunting's poems at a time when few others were—and for many years Bunting's reputation (such as it was) rested upon them. In later life he dropped *They say Etna* from his *Collected Poems* and added a note to *The Complaint of the Morpethshire Farmer*: 'The War and the Forestry Commission have outdated this complaint.' From Coldside and Spylaw (and

COQUETDALE SHEEP DOG TRIALS.

Competitors (upper picture) in the Coquetdale Sheep Dog Trials, held at Rothbury on Saturday. Below are seen Mr J. M. Wilson, of Holmshaw, with his International winner Fly, and a group of officials, with Mr T. O. Donkin (hon. secretary) in centre.

Competitors and officials seen at the Coquetdale Sheep Dog Trials held at Rothbury, Saturday 6 October 1928. J.M. Wilson is pictured left with his International winner Fly.
From the *Newcastle Journal and North Star*, Monday 8 October, 1928.

from nearby Chartners, where Bunting stayed when 'Ned' Wilson could no longer accommodate him) can be seen the massed ranks of Harwood Forest where afforestation began in the 1930s; and where once there were rolling Northumbrian Hills.

This period of Northumbrian experience came back to him at a key moment in *Briggflatts* when 'Then is diffused in Now':

> Shepherds follow the links,
> sweet turf studded with thrift;
> fell-born men of precise instep
> leading demure dogs
> from Tweed and Till and Teviotdale,
> with hair combed back from the muzzle,
> dogs from Redesdale and Coquetdale
> taught by Wilson or Telfer.
> Their teeth are white as birch,
> slow under black fringe
> of silent, accurate lips

Here again, the specific details of this part of Northumberland are recalled: '*Wilson* was less known than *Telfer,*' we are told in a note, 'but not less skilful'. Was Bunting actually present at the Rothbury trials of October 1928 where J.M. Wilson of Moffat (no relation to Bunting's host, Ned) beat the champion of previous years, Walter Telfer?

Moving on

Bunting was soon on the move again: first to Italy, where he worked with Pound again. The 1930s were for Bunting, like many people in the North, a period of great financial uncertainty. He was constantly on the move, rarely staying long in one place, always on the lookout for cheaper lodgings or for a way of supporting himself and his newly acquired wife, Marian Culver. In a postscript to a letter to Ezra Pound in 1930 he writes: 'By the way, I got married to that American girl I was with in Venice. She comes from Eau Claire.' His mother visited the couple at Rapallo, and his Jesmond neighbour, the musicologist Whittaker, became a presence at the Rapallo concerts which Bunting helped Ezra Pound to organise. The musical significance of these concerts, which included some of the earliest resurrections of baroque musicians such as Vivaldi and (in Whittaker's editions) William Young, has yet to be fully researched, and Bunting's achievement in them remains to be fully acknowledged. In time Bunting became aware of the need to distance himself from Pound's influence as Pound's political views became increasingly maniacally fascist: he left to live for a while in the Canaries (where he is rumoured to have played chess with Franco). It was a time of unhappiness and poverty for him and his young family: in 1937 his wife left him and took their first two children back to America with her. He never saw his son Rustam, who was born later in that year.

Late in 1937 Bunting was back in England. He bought a boat called the *Thistle* for a hundred pounds in which he wintered on the South Devon coast (he was later to sell it for two hundred pounds). The following year he spent sailing in the

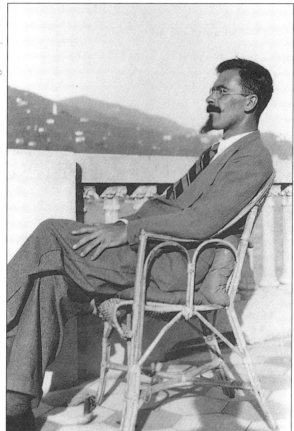

Basil Bunting Poetry Archive

far left: Basil Bunting, Marian and Annie Bunting photographed in Rapallo, February 1931.

left: Basil Bunting at around the same time, probably taken on the balcony of the poet W.B. Yeats' apartment in Rapallo.

Mediterranean. To gain more knowledge of seamanship, Bunting returned to Newcastle in 1938 to attend Nellist's Nautical School which was situated at 10 Summerhill Terrace, Rye Hill. This school was formed in 1928 by William and George Nellist and closed around 1959. Bunting was to describe it as a very peculiar place, a cramming school for those who wanted certificates to be mates or masters. It was said to have turned out nearly half of all the Merchant Navy Officers in Britain. Bunting describes the atmosphere: 'When I first saw it I couldn't believe my eyes. I walked in asking for Mr. Nellist and was shown into a room in an old house across which I couldn't see because of the thickness of the tobacco smoke—all these men smoking pipes. No window was ever opened, the smoke just accumulated and got thicker and thicker like London fog ... You learned the routine things, how to handle the nautical tables and the theory of navigation and so forth. I picked and chose. Because of my eyes I couldn't hold a certificate, so that didn't enter into the matter at all. I just wanted to know enough to handle a boat intelligently.' He went on to describe how Mr Nellist described the ways of correcting the the error of a sextant: 'Now, ye dinna need to knaw much aboot it, cause it's out a date. And if the examiner say to ye, what aboot the angle off the arc, ye just say to that Board of Trade Examiner, bugger the angle off the arc, there's a new method.'

Dick Keys, an ex-Nellist student of a slightly later period, gives us further insight into Nellist's Nautical School in an unpublished memoir: 'The school was run by the two Nellist brothers one of whom was called Jacky. He was a slim schoolmaster type, the other, Billy, a portly gentleman who always seemed to have a spattering of cigarette ash on his waistcoat. Legend had it that neither had any seafaring qualifications. The explanation for this singular omission was that both had failed their Board of Trade eyesight tests which were *de rigueur* for anyone pursuing a career at sea. Whether true or not they certainly ran a very successful establishment which attracted pupils from all over the world. They were assisted by a Captain Tate (or Tait) and an ex-Royal Navy yeoman of signals who taught Morse code and semaphore signalling.' He also describes the interior of the building which complements Bunting's account. 'My recollection of the interior of 10 Summerhill Terrace is of cold (it was winter time) and darkness. The lower half of all the walls were painted olive green and above that a buff colour. In what must have been the front room on the ground floor, where I did most of my studying; there was a small open fire which once in a while one of the brothers would keep alive with a small shovel full of coal. What was lacking in comfort was made up by the quality of the tuition. There were no fixed terms. A pupil could begin his course at any time—in effect whenever your boat came in, which was a boon to seafarers.

'As everyone started at different times everyone was working at different levels. This seemed to create no great problems. The brothers just circulated around the classroom helping and advising the students as they did so. Formal, whole class tuition was not very frequent. A technique much used was practising examination questions culled from previous examinations.'

Bunting was to follow this experience by becoming a skipper of a millionaire's schooner visiting

Canada and the USA—his friend Louis Zukofsky recalled him turning up in New York with a sextant under his arm.

With the impending outbreak of war Bunting made his way back to England from America eager to enlist, arriving in Northumberland on May Day 1939. Like his Objectivist colleague George Oppen, he was eager to fight in this war. He was later to describe his change in attitude: 'During the First World War it was possible to believe, I did believe, that it was a totally unnecessary war fought for purely selfish ends, to get hold of markets and things like that. You couldn't believe that, in the second one at all. It was perfectly obvious for years beforehand that nothing short of war and violence would ever stop Hitler and his appalling career.'

Bunting could get no work on his return save for some WEA classes at Morpeth in Northumberland, in December 1939—six lectures on History from Alexander the Great to the Middle Ages—so he had to live off his mother. He was unable to get into any of the service units until he came across a doctor who had known his father, and it seems that he allowed Bunting to learn the eye test by heart. By this means he was able to enter the Royal Air Force. Although considered to be too old for active service, he eventually became a 'balloon man' in charge of a squad of Welshmen, many of whom did not speak English. After training he was sent to a balloon site in Hull which he found very boring. After volunteering for 'dangerous and difficult work at sea' he found himself in a job that was in fact the most comfortable that you could find in the Royal Air Force: escorting convoys with balloons in the North Sea on a converted millionaire's yacht, *The Golden Hind*. Conditions on board, he recalled, were so good that it was extremely difficult to get anybody to take a day off when they had a day in harbour. He was based near Leven, Methil, Fife and when not at sea he was having his poems typed up by a young local secretary, to whom he dedicated what sounds like his farewell to poetry: *To Violet, with prewar poems*: 'These traces from a world that's dead …'

Late in 1941 Bunting was posted to Rosyth for a six week driving course, and from there he volunteered for service in Persia. In a letter to the Air Ministry he said he knew old, medieval, classical Persian—they were sufficiently impressed that they sent him as an interpreter to a squadron in Persia. Bunting had learned Persian in order to read Firdausi: 'but I never [he recalled in a later interview] expected to hear it spoken or speak a word of it! In fact, I didn't hear a word of it spoken until I arrived in Persia and was called upon to interpret for a court martial. You can imagine how difficult that was. I hope they put the right man in jail. Very fortunately it wasn't one of those cases where it would require shooting or hanging.'

Bunting's war and his career in Persia after the war lie outside the scope of this book, though this period of danger and adventure were of immense importance to him. He rose rapidly through the ranks of the RAF and finished the war as Squadron Leader and Vice-Consul of Isfahan. He told Peter Quartermain in 1971: 'The war did me a lot of good; it gave me confidence, assurance in myself as man of action; it gave me power of decision under great responsibility. It gave me authority: I learned my Wing-Commander-act.'

This career of excitement, and later secret service, ended abruptly in 1948 when he married his second wife, Sima Alladadian. Bunting and Sima returned to England for a six week long honeymoon. Faced with the prospect of unemployment he was relieved when in April 1949, *The Times* offered him a job as their special correspondent in Teheran for a year. Sima-Maria Bunting, their first child was born there in 1950.

In April 1950 *The Times* job came to an end and in May Bunting and his young family returned to England and stayed with his mother in Throckley. He was then offered a job by a syndicate of provincial newspapers, as their foreign correspondent to Italy; this job was soon curtailed by a shortage of newsprint. In June 1951 they returned home to Throckley and Bunting was again faced with the prospect of looking for work. In October of 1951 he returned to Teheran for a further period as correspondent for *The Times*.

Basil Bunting's financial column under the banner headline
Finance by our CITY experts
from the *Evening Chronicle*, Thursday 13 November, 1958.

Today's prices

LONDON NOON
BRITISH FUNDS
Consol 2½ p.c. ....50⅞ (−⅛)
Savings 2½ p.c. .....82 7/16 (+1/16)
War Loan 3½ p.c. ...65 11/16 (−1/16)

INDUSTRIALS, ETC.
British Alum. ....60s 4½d (+1s 4½d)
Berger ....6s 6d (−3d)
Borax ....15s 6d (−3d)
British Oxygen ....45s (−3d)
English China ....45s 9d (−3d)
Forestal Land ....16s 9d (−3d)
International Nickel ......162 (+1)
London Brick ......58s 11½d (+3d)
Pinchin Johnson ......21s 9d (−6d)
Tate and Lyle .....70s 9d (+4½d)
Unilever ....100s 3d (−3d)

ENGINEERING, ETC.
A.E.I. ....57s (+3d)
J. Brown ....31s 7½d (−3d)
Consett ....20s 6d (−3d)
Dorman Long ....25s (−3d)
E.M.I. ....53s 9d (+3d)
English Elect. ....57s (−3d)
Rediffusion ......36s 9d (+6d)
Stewarts and Lloyds ......25s (−11½d)
B.M.C. ....13s (−4½d)
Lucas ....43s 9d (−6d)
Hawker ....30s 9d (+6d)
British and Commonwealth 43s 6d (+3d)

STORES, ETC.
Allied Bakeries ....38s 9d (−3d)
Bovril ....58s 9d (+3d)
Lyons ....72s (+3d)
Woolworth ....49s 6d (−3d)
Courtaulds ......29s 9d (+10½d)
Calicos ....34s 9d (−1s)
Horrocks ....26s (−2s 9d)
Distillers ....29s 9d (+3d)
Imps ....49s 6d (−3d)

OILS, ETC.
Canadian Eagle ....62s 9d (+3s 6d)
Shell ....162s 3d (+1s 7½d)
Ultramar ....90s (+3d)
Harties ......65s 9d (+1s 4½d)
Ofsits ....76s 7½d (+7½d)

ALTHOUGH business is not quite so brisk, the tone is satisfactory, Stock Markets being helped by the good showing made by the October trade figures and the continued firm advices from Wall Street.

The gilt-edged market was a shade hesitant while awaiting the bank rate decision. The rate is unchanged at 4½ per cent. and was in accordance with general expectations.

Industrial blue chips keep steady to firm. Foods and furnishings hold steady. Steels are hardly affected by the further fall in steel production, while general engineering show a few irregular changes. One or two shipping shares are better.

Homecoming

In April 1952 Bunting was expelled from Persia by Mossadeq, the Iranian premier who had just succeeded in nationalising the huge British oil holdings in Iran, and who was about to embark on his struggle for power with the Shah. Bunting travelled to England by car, a journey that took a month, with Sima and daughter Maria. By June they had reached his mother in Throckley but Bunting was again experiencing great difficulty finding work, as he was now no longer *The Times* correspondent in Persia. In November Thomas Faramaz was born, adding to his financial responsibilities. Back at his mother's house, he began to realise that the skills which had made him valued and authoritative in Persia were not appreciated in 1950s Britain. Over fifty, without formal qualifications (though he had sufficient real experience to publish an impressive *curriculum vitae* listing his achievements), there was little chance of a suitable job to support himself, his young wife, and his two young children. In September 1953 he managed to get some part-time work with the *Manchester Guardian*, for which he was paid at a low rate, and did some proof-reading for the NCB publication *Mining*.

In a long typewritten letter to his erstwhile patron, Margaret de Silver, he writes of his predicament: 'Things here—I mean our personal affairs seem to be very close to a climax. We spent the last few days entirely without money and with very little to eat, though we managed to feed the babies. Mother has run her overdraft to the limit the bank will allow: it is secured on her house and she is being pressed to sell the house to pay the bank its five hundred pounds. Meanwhile I've been applying for "National Assistance"—the new name for outdoor relief. They are not polite and I doubt whether we will get it. We have not sold Sima's engagement ring nor my irreplaceable Persian and Arabic books, and I am still nominally owner of a car, or the rusty remains of one, which the customs will not let me sell; and they cannot even make up their minds how much duty they mean to charge on it. It is clear that the car will not fetch even the minimum they can charge—they have caused it to lie rusting for over a year. Unfortunately our National Assistance area is the Marxist stronghold hereabouts—Blaydon—and we are bourgeois parasites, or so I gather.

I had been led to believe several times during the past ten years that I had deserved well of my country in a small way, and eighteen months ago half the papers in the country were praising me for my work in Persia—just after Mosaddeq chucked me out. But in that time I have earned only about ten pounds.'

During this period the neglect of the literary world affected him deeply, and he wrote little and published less. His *Poems 1950* (published by a Texan little press while he was in Persia) sunk with little recognition outside a small circle of poets, and plans to publish him in this country were still-born.

On 26 July 1954 Bunting finally obtained regular work as a sub-editor at

The offices of the *Newcastle Evening Chronicle* in 1965, shortly before Basil Bunting's retirement.

Newcastle Chronicle & Journal Ltd.

Basil Bunting at the Newcastle Chronicle Offices in the 1960s. He is writing in one of his poetry notebooks. From his early teens his eyesight was a cause for concern—on his Leighton Park medical form his father was to record that his eyes were not normal and that he required glasses. By the 1960s there was a marked deterioration and he was to experience difficulty proof-reading his editorial copy. After a cataract operation in 1967 his eyesight improved.

the *Newcastle Daily Journal* and was able to bring home a steady salary. He worked on the evening-shift from 5pm to 2am six days a week after which he would travel back to Throckley on his moped. The local wildlife fascinated him: 'That was worth doing. In the middle of the night you saw all sorts of creatures on that road that you never see in the daytime. Every kind of owl I got familiar with, and foxes carrying chickens in their mouths, and things of that sort. It was very nice in some ways, of course you were terribly tired, a tiring business being up all night working on a newspaper and then trying to sleep when everyone else is up and about in the day.' And on one prophetic occasion he listened to a bull lowing in a nearby field. 'The bull I noticed one day at a farm near Throckley where I was living at the moment; and you know, it struck me, at once, nobody has noticed the bull has a *tenor* voice.' This led directly—about a decade later—to the now famous opening line of Briggflatts: 'Brag sweet tenor bull'. His keen naturalist's eye is evident throughout his work, of course—as in his description of a falcon from *The Spoils* of 1951, recording an unforgettable sight:

> Have you seen a falcon stoop
> accurate, unforseen
> and absolute, between
> wind-ripples over harvest? Dread
> of what's to be, is and has been—
> were we not better dead?

> His wings churn air
> to flight.
> Feathers alight
> with sun, he rises where
> dazzle rebuts our stare,
> wonder our fright.

Sima and the children left for a long vacation in Persia in the October of 1956. In 1957 he began work on the day-shift of the sister paper the *Evening Chronicle* which offered more congenial hours, and he was to remain in this job until 30 August 1966, when he retired. In May of 1957 Bunting and his mother moved to Shadingfield, a house in the nearby village of Wylam, and were joined there in June by Sima and the family.

Bunting is remembered by a colleague on the 'subs' bench as an unassuming man, with a good financial brain. He was responsible for, among other things, the financial page with its listing of the movement of stocks and shares: 'he could always tell you where to put your money!' A popular man, he told stories of his time in Persia and how he had had to leave while correspondent for *The Times*. He was always writing, and fellow journalists were aware of his poetry, although he was also known for his humour—the story is told of a local councillor who had risen to the rank of Major during the war—a fact that he regularly reminded the local press of, when they reported on him. On one occasion he rang the *Evening Chronicle* and was put through to Bunting: 'WING COMMANDER BUNTING here,' said Basil, with impressive solemnity.

On fine days he was to be found eating his lunch in the nearby St John's churchyard; on wet days he was likely to be found in the Lit and Phil as there was a special arrangement with *The Journal* and *Evening Chronicle* to allow reporters to use the reading room of the library, which was directly opposite *The Journal and Chronicle* offices. It is fair to say that Bunting found his work as a journalist stultifying, and had some unkind words for his fellow journalists: '... Provincial journalists are not capable of any thought of any sort at all.' From his earliest days as a London hack journalist in the 1920s he had maintained his disrespect for the profession. In a letter to to his twelve-year-old Throckley cousin Billy Swann in 1927, he had written:

'I sometimes see people playing [tennis] on the hard courts in Lincoln's Inn Fields when I am on my way to the dusty offices of dreary editors in Fleet Street, who say "Nothing today, thankyou" as though I were a peddlar selling bootlaces instead of the Celebrated Mr Bunting trying to sell articles. but sometimes they print things and then the chief troubles are:-
(a)   that they don't pay enough.
(b)   that they don't pay at all unless you go round and bother them.
(c)   they always choose the bad articles instead of the good ones, and the worse an article is the surer they are to stick your name at the bottom of it in big letters so that you get a bad reputation instead of a good one.
I am going to ask a bargee to take me to Harwich on his barge so that I can write about it in the papers, but don't know whether he will take me. He may say "Alright. That'll be a pound" and I can't afford that. If I go and do it I'll send you the article. It might be amusing.'

His preoccupation with money, as his dislike of journalism, is as relevant in the 1950s and 1960s as it was in the 1920s.

He nevertheless used this period as a journalist in Newcastle to keep writing, filling notebooks on the train ride from Newcastle to Wylam. One young poet who worked alongside him in his last years at the *Chronicle* was Barry MacSweeney, a cub journalist at the time. MacSweeney recalled showing an early poem to Bunting, and getting a direct lesson in Bunting's approach to editing poems, as opposed to journalism: 'showed Bunting "Walk" poem, it came back sliced down to about four lines and a note: start again from there'. MacSweeney also recalls Bunting teaching him to work out the tide tables after MacSweeney had published incorrect low water times and safe crossings to

Lindisfarne, with near disastrous consequences: 'You have always got to be accurate,' said the older poet to the younger.

It has been generally understood that Bunting lived in comparative obscurity during the 1950s, so much so that the American poet Robert Creeley, on a visit to Newcastle in 1964, expressed surprise that Bunting was still alive, and living locally. However, some people did venture north to visit: in December 1956 the poet Gael Turnbull, one of Bunting's earliest and most consistent supporters, made his way to Throckley to see Bunting: 'It was his mother's home, a fairly substantial terraced house. Sima and the two children were in Persia … up some high steps, to an ordinary door, any door. With a man to open the door, to say, "Yes, I am …" and to greet me. A little amused perhaps at my obvious surprise that he existed. How could it be? And how could it be otherwise? my first bizarre reaction: how much he was the story-book image of a scout-master. Then, another image of dignity and humour.' Bunting on reading this account later, was to remark of the 'scout-master': 'that would be the Wing-Commander Bunting.'

The Roman Wall at Cuddy's Crag c.1940. This section of the Roman Wall at its most spectacular was one of Bunting's particular favourites and featured in his ten most important sights in the region.

Recognition

In the summer of 1964 another young Newcastle poet, Tom Pickard, took the advice of Jonathan Williams, American poet and publisher associated with Black Mountain College, and contacted Bunting for the first time. That a young Newcastle poet should discover his Newcastle mentor by way of North Carolina is, perhaps, a significant indicator of the obscurity in which Bunting lived. He set in motion the events which were to lead to Bunting's triumphant rediscovery of poetry. Pickard recorded the circumstances of this first meeting in 1979:

'One Sunday night shortly after receiving Jonathan's letter. I decided to look up Mr Bunting in the telephone directory, and I gave him a ring from a public box. His Persian wife Sima answered the call, then sent Basil to the phone. Nervously I explained that I was putting together a magazine and wanted some contributions from him. He invited me over, and I caught the next train out.'

Pickard was to prove the catalyst that transformed Bunting's life. Over the following year Bunting wrote—in some ways as an object lesson for Pickard—the final long poem, *Briggflatts*, upon which his public reputation was founded.

Tom Pickard and his wife Connie were also instrumental in bringing about the Newcastle poetry revival of the mid-1960s and the 1970s. The *Evening Chronicle*, 12 June 1964, declared 'There's poetry within the old city walls.' The article went on to describe how 'Newcastle's ancient city wall will become the centre of modern poetry for the area if an 18-year-old youth's scheme proves successful. Thomas Pickard of Buston Terrace, Jesmond has rented the famous Morden Tower from Newcastle Corporation for 10 shillings a week and is busily turning it into a bookroom where he plans to stage exhibitions and poetry readings.' Pickard was quoted as saying that he had installed bookshelves and: 'I sell books, mainly of modern poetry which is not obtainable in most bookshops … Friends from the Art School have helped by designing posters, and I am hoping to have regular reading sessions by modern poets.' Significantly it also said that he had plans to produce a magazine, published from the Morden Tower: 'which will contain contributions from North-country poets.'

Briggflatts which was to become Bunting's most famous poem is described, in the notes that Bunting appended to the main text, as 'An autobiography, but not a record of fact. The first movement is no more a chronicle than the third. The truth of the poem is of another kind.' It is nevertheless one of the most enduring embodiments of his northerness, and contains descriptive passages that capture the sense of continuity and

Tom Pickard, June 1964, around the time when he first met Basil Bunting.

Morden Tower in 1967. Tom and Connie Pickard took out a lease on the tower on 30 March 1964, and quickly set about creating the book-room which was used for readings and discussions. They sold books of poetry that could not be had elsewhere, but—above all—they created the Newcastle poetry revival of the late 1960s which is still continuing today. Basil Bunting gave many memorable readings here including the first public reading of *Briggflatts*.

renewal which he found within the Northumbrian landscape. Bunting was irritated by a public that sought explanation, and made this clear in *A Note on Briggflatts*, Durham 1989: '*Briggflatts* is a poem: it needs no explanation. The sound of the words spoken aloud is itself the meaning, just as the sound of the notes played on the proper instruments is the meaning of any piece of music.'

Bunting read *Briggflatts* publicly for the first time at the Morden Tower Bookroom on 22 December 1965. The *Evening Chronicle* recorded the event, adding: '*Briggflatts* is to be published in America next month [in *Poetry (Chicago)*] and in Britain in February. This long poem has met with great attention already, though this is the first public reading of it in the North.' On its publication by Fulcrum Press, Tom Pickard reviewed it for the *Evening Chronicle* on 26 February 1966. Other acclaim for *Briggflatts* followed from an increasingly wide range of critics, and from this point Bunting's reputation at least—if not his fortune—became secure.

There are now many critical studies and descriptions of *Briggflatts*: and this is not the place for another. Briefly the poem is rich in detail (cut down from an alleged 2000 lines to around 700), lyrical power and memory—and for our purposes, it is a poem deeply rooted in the North of England. Bunting describes a lifetime's journey away from youthful love, throughout a wandering youth, towards a gradual return to an 'acknowledged land'—the land of St Cuthbert and the Lindisfarne Gospels, of people who were 'comfortable and easy to deal with', with Throckley soft rolled 'r's in their speech.

Briggflatts was followed by a long overdue *Collected Poems* in 1968, which cemented his reputation, and established the canon of his poems which is maintained today. In the remaining years of his life he was to add only a few but significant short poems.

Also in 1968 Bunting received the newly established Northern Arts Literary Fellowship at the Universities of Durham and Newcastle. Although one senior Durham academic is reported as saying 'Who's Basil Bunting?' on his appointment, this Fellowship served to emphasise the growing regard in which the region held him. He saw students regularly, and directed them—sometimes forcefully—on their apprentice writing. He printed a page of advice embodying the wisdom of half a century of experience—and advised them on how best to develop their poetic voice: one student from the south (Wilko Johnson of the rock group Doctor Feelgood) asked which 'southrons' wrote well. 'Keats', said Bunting after some thought, 'Keats is for Cockneys.'

I SUGGEST

1. Compose aloud; poetry is a sound.
2. Vary rhythm enough to stir the emotion you want but not so as to lose impetus.
3. Use spoken words and syntax.
4. Fear adjectives; they bleed nouns. Hate the passive.
5. Jettison ornament gaily but keep shape

Put your poem away till you forget it, then:
6. Cut out every word you dare.
7. Do it again a week later, and again.

Never explain --- your reader is as smart as you.

Above: *I Suggest*, Basil Bunting's advice to student poets, typeset and printed on an Adana press in the early 1970s.

Above right: Basil Bunting and the poet Allen Ginsberg in Tom and Connie Pickard's flat in Eslington Terrace, Jesmond, Newcastle upon Tyne 22 May 1965. Allen Armstrong writing in the *Sunday Sun* 23 May 1965 described the scene: 'Mr Bunting, a Newcastle journalist, and one of Britain's foremost modern poets, was sitting at the time, on the settee next to Ginsberg. America's original "Angel-headed hipster" flopped forward and lay with his head in Bunting's lap. He giggled. Bunting smiled. The young admirers laughed.'

Below right: City Hall 2 June 1966. Basil Bunting is seen here with Boris Brott conducting the Northern Sinfonia Orchestra and David Haslam, flute. Bunting read his poems with the music of Vivaldi, Corelli and Albinoni. During rehearsals in April 1966, Bunting was testing a loudspeaker system in the City Hall: 'I will be reading some of my poems, of course, at the concert [he told an *Evening Chronicle* reporter]. But not being a trained opera singer, I cannot throw my voice softly. That is why mechanical aid is needed. Otherwise I think I would manage all right. I used to have to bawl orders at 600 men in South Africa during the war [en route to the Middle East], and I was for a time a sailor as well and used to plenty of hailing.'

As President of Northern Arts (1974-76) he argued repeatedly for increased payments to local poets: a late Ode recalls Tom Pickard's failure to get a decent living as a poet:

What the Chairman Told Tom

Poetry? It's a hobby.
I run model trains.
Mr Shaw there breeds pigeons.

It's not work. You dont sweat.
Nobody pays for it.
You *could* advertise soap.

Art, that's opera; or repertory
The Desert Song.
Nancy was in the Chorus.

But to ask for twelve pounds a week
married, aren't you?
you've got a nerve.

How could I look a bus conductor
in the face
if I paid you twelve pounds?

Who says it's poetry, anyhow?
My ten year old
can do it *and* rhyme

I get three thousand and expenses,
a car, vouchers,
but I'm an accountant.

They do what I tell them,
my company.
What do *you* do?

Nasty little words, nasty long words,
it's unhealthy.
I want to wash when I meet a poet.

They're Reds, addicts,
all delinquents.
What you write is rot.

Mr Hines says so, and he's a schoolteacher,
he ought to know.
Go and find *work*.

Newcastle Chronicle & Journal Ltd.

Basil Bunting, and the poets Barry MacSweeney, Stuart Montgomery, Tony Harrison at the Haymarket Hotel, Percy Street, Newcastle upon Tyne 1970.

Basil Bunting and the American poet Allen Ginsberg beside the village cross at Bywell, Northumberland, c.1972. It is not surprising that Ginsberg would be taken to visit one of Bunting's significant places.

Increasingly the Grand Old Man of literature, he gave sharp and pungent interviews. One interviewer asked what the ten most important sights in the region were. He replied: 'The moors; Durham Cathedral; Brigflatts Meeting House (and Dentdale in passing); the Bewcastle Cross; the Farne Islands, seen from Bamburgh to Seahouses; the Roman Wall between the Twice Brewed and the Mile Castle public houses; the two churches at Bywell; the valley of the North Tyne; the beech

Basil Bunting and Richard Caddel at the launch of *The Selected Poems of Joseph Skipsey*, Sunderland Arts Centre 1976.

avenue at Capheaton; and the Isabella pit heap at Throckley.[7]

It is possible to trace Bunting's associations with each of these in turn.

Two late Odes are closely associated with the region: the celebratory poem for the Tercentenary of Brigflatts Meeting House, a Quaker celebration of the silence and beauty of the place itself, and a bright lyric *Stones trip Coquet Burn* with a tongue twisting Welsh rhyme scheme, set in the landscape of Bunting's Simonside experiences of the 1920s. In each poem, the old man is celebrating the dynamism of his Northumbrian home place. 'Look' he wrote 'how clouds dance / under the wind's wing, and leaves / delight in transience.' It is worth adding that even his translation of the Persian children's poem *The Pious Cat*—worked on from 1937 to 1977—turns the royal Persian cat into a Haltwhistle barnyard tabby.

In the 1970s Bunting edited two collections of poems. Both were acts of piety towards significant elders in his life: *Selected Poems of Ford Madox Ford* appeared in 1971 followed by *Selected Poems of Joseph Skipsey* which was published by Ceolfrith Press, Sunderland in 1976. The latter was a return to his roots and a celebration of a poet of the Northumbrian mining tradition. It was a personal selection intended for pleasure and not a scholarly work. Bunting could not resist a note of his own family history: 'Skipsey lived to be 71. His wife died more than a year before him, and the dignified, rather austere old man was cared for by his housekeeper, a granddaughter, Jane Skipsey, just twelve years old. His son William was inspector of schools at Durham, his eldest son James, master shifter at the Montague Colliery at Scotswood [he was also Manager of Montague Fireclay Colliery c.1906], where Joseph Skipsey sometimes visited my father, the colliery doctor there; but I was too young to have any memory of him.' The Skipsey selection had been in his mind from as early as 1930, when he wrote to T.S. Eliot from Brooklyn, New York: ' ... for a number of years I have wanted to get somebody to make an edition of Skipsey's poems. Skipsey died about 1902, very old.

Basil Bunting and Stuart Montgomery at a Colpitts Poetry Reading in Durham, October 1976.

Most of his life he was a working miner. He wrote a fair volume of poems with a very distinct personality. Some of them were what one might expect—copies lacking some of the impulse of the original: chief influences, Burns, Heine and Blake. But quite a large number are direct, uninfluenced, and thoroughly worth reading, and half a dozen very short lyrics deserve to be as well known as any lyric poetry. During his lifetime Rossetti tried to get him recognised, but Skipsey's own bristling character prevented it. Somebody—I think it was Gosse—wrote a preface for an edition of *Carols, Songs and Ballads* made somewhere about 1889 by Walter Scott of Felling. This edition has been unobtainable for years and there has been no other. I wasn't able to discover who owns the copyright. Scott's liquidators or executors didn't answer my letters. I don't want to claim too much for Skipsey. He was a minor poet. I don't think his book would sell at all quickly, but it ought to sell steadily, because the poems are as fresh now as in the seventies; and particularly it should have a local sale in Northumberland. A good many of the ballads are in Northumberland dialect.' Once again we are made aware that even when he was far away from the region, culturally, the region remained close in his thoughts.

After this Bunting finished little—he researched material on the Rising of the North in the Lit and Phil in the 1970s. Though notes for a last poem exist, he was unable to finish it to his satisfaction. He lived on his own—in Washington New Town, in Jonathan Williams' house in Dentdale, and in Greystead, on the North Tyne, where he was happy to be in the heart of his favourite landscape. Here he once more watched wildlife ('Did I tell you about the cats? The snake-and-lizard man [poet and naturalist Colin Simms] came to see me, hunting a lizard said to have been seen in Northumberland, where it had no business to be. I mentioned casually the wild cats (Felix Sylvestris) now plentiful in the border forests. He got enormously excited, got on his motor-bicycle and rushed off to the forest, where he found three wild cats in a single evening. Apparently none of the farmers or forestry people had ever thought of mentioning wild cats to the naturalists …') and entertained the growing stream of admirers who came from all over the world to visit him. He jotted fitfully, and accumulated notes towards work celebrating Linnaeus, the new moon, and his old Ackworth friend Cooper Stephenson—few of these drafts were ever circulated, though one, *Such syllables flicker out of grass,* was handprinted by Bunting (on the same press he had used for his advice for young poets) and circulated to friends in 1972. The compression and complexity of this poem—reminiscent of his friend Louis Zukofsky—suggest that he was about to enter on a new phase in his composition. The language is rich in the sounds and shapes of his northern surroundings … 'Light stots from stone, sets ridge and kerf quick / as shot skims rust from steel', rich in historical detail, gleaned from his reading in the Lit and Phil on the Rising of the North.

Sadly the strength to continue deserted him—in conversation with Jonathan Williams towards the end of his life he was asked how the new long poem he was writing was going: 'Stuck. S-T-U-C-K.' Nevertheless, he remained physically strong and active, and enjoying walks and whisky right up to his death. Shortly before his death he moved to Whitley Chapel, just south of Hexham, and fretted because he'd lost the wonderful surroundings of the North Tyne. Although his health was gradually failing, his mind and voice remained sound: visitors a few days before his death recall him reciting the works of the early Scots poet Gavin Douglas from memory with strength and vigour.

Bunting died after a short illness in Hexham General Hospital on 17 April 1985. Tom Pickard as always was generous in his tribute: 'Basil was a great friend to budding poets and gave me incredible encouragement. He was so vigorous and agile, we thought he must have made some pact so as not to die. Even though he was 85 his death has come as a terrible shock to us all. We thought he was immortal. In the 1960s he helped to make the Tower famous, influencing many of us with his incredible craftsmanship and professionalism. It was because of Basil that we were able to attract all the best poets to Newcastle.'

His ashes lie near a simple tombstone in the Quaker graveyard at Brigflatts. A more public memorial in Durham University Botanic Gardens quotes from *Briggflatts*:

> Words!
> Pens are too light.
> Take a chisel to write.

At Brigflatts Burial Ground 1986, from a photograph by Raymond Moore (1920-1987).

Chronology

The starting point for any record of Bunting's life is the *curriculum vitae* that he prepared on his return from Persia in 1952. Since that time Garth Clucas has produced an outline chronology and more recently Peter Quartermain has added much new information.

Basil Bunting and his sister Joyce with their Aunts Hettie and Sallie Bunting, in a snapshot photograph taken probably by Thomas Lowe Bunting around 1910.

Basil Bunting and his sister Joyce from an experimental photographic postcard taken by Thomas Lowe Bunting, and sent to his sister Hettie in Edgbaston, Birmingham from Scotswood at 8.30pm on 18 April 1910.

1863 November 9, Sarah Anna Bunting (*Auntie Sallie*—Thomas Lowe's sister) born, (died 21 July 1946). There was another sister, Harriet Alice *Auntie Hettie*, of whom little is known except that she and Sarah Anna were both spinsters.

1868 April 6, Thomas Lowe Bunting, MD, FRS born, the son of Joseph Bunting a draper of Taghill, Heanor, Derbyshire and Mary Bunting formerly Lowe of Burton-on-Trent, Staffordshire.

1875 23 July, Annie Cheesman born, the daughter of Isaac Taylor Cheesman a mining engineer of Throckley, Northumberland and Annie Cheesman formerly Forster (died 11 July 1969).

1895 T.L. Bunting living at 17 Prospect Terrace, Scotswood-on-Tyne.

1898 1 November, T.L. Bunting marries Annie Cheesman.

1899 T.L. Bunting and Annie move to 27 Denton Road, Scotswood-on-Tyne.

1900 1 March, Basil Bunting born at Scotswood-on-Tyne, christened Basil Cheesman Bunting. It is likely that Bunting was born at 27 Denton Road. In view of the fact that in 1916, T.L. Bunting filled in Bunting's medical form ('It is requested that the following questions may be answered by the medical man who usually has attended the boy') on his entry to Leighton Park, it is reasonable to assume that he was present at the birth of his son.

1902 Joyce Lowe Bunting born.

1903 Marian Culver (to be his wife) born, Eau Claire, Wisconsin.

1906 Attends Miss A.M. Bell's *Kindergarten*. Miss A.M. Bell ran a school at 24 West Parade, (Rye Hill) just off Westmoreland Road; she is listed in the local Directories for 1907/8. His favourite books were Grimms' Fairy Tales and books by E. Nesbitt and Beatrix Potter.

1909-1911 Royal Grammar School, Newcastle upon Tyne (There is no evidence in Royal Grammar School records to support this claim).

c.1912 Learns rock-climbing with his father and the Abraham brothers in the Lake District.

1912-16 Ackworth School, near Pontefract, Yorkshire (a Quaker School). During this time he was an avid cyclist and apparently known for taking long unauthorised rides. (In Ackworth

Isaac Taylor Cheesman JP c.1914, Basil Bunting's grandfather. A miner and mining engineer, and at the time a retired colliery manager and agent.

Thomas Lowe Bunting from a passport photograph taken in the early 1920s.

records there is a reference to a boy being killed cycling downhill in 1918, so it is possible that Bunting had his bicycle with him at Ackworth).

1913   First visit to Brigflatts. (Bunting was himself unclear as to when he first went there, though he is believed to have spent several holidays staying with the Greenbank family. Evidence in unpublished correspondence suggests that after 1915 he was not to return again until 1965).

1914   Autumn, T.L. Bunting appointed Radiologist to the Northumberland War Hospital at Gosforth.

1916   September, enters Leighton Park School, Reading, Berkshire (a Quaker School).

1916   24 October, letter from T.L. Bunting to the Headmaster of Leighton Park from 38 Moorside, Fenham. Written at a time when Bunting was expressing discontent with the school.

1917   December, leaves Leighton Park School and returns, presumably, to 95 Jesmond Road, Jesmond, Newcastle upon Tyne. (What was he doing during the weeks before his Tribunal?)

1918   16 March, 2256 Bunting, Basil C. age 18 **Tribunal** Preliminary examination by the National Service Representative, 26 Northumberland Street, Newcastle upon Tyne.

1918   17 April, **Newcastle Military Tribunal.**

1918   20 June, Newcastle Panel of the Northumberland Appeal Tribunal.

1918   December, *The Leightonian* 'serving 112 days…'

1918-19   In the Register for the 1918-19 Elections T.L. Bunting is living at 95 Jesmond Road.

1919   Released from Winchester on sick-leave, and simply does not return. There are no extant records to support this claim: both Wormwood Scrubs and Winchester Prisons have no records of Bunting being imprisoned there.

1920   Enrolls at the London School of Economics.

1920   T.L. Bunting at 6 Portland Terrace.

1922   Leaves London School of Economics without taking a degree. Briefly becomes secretary to Harry Barnes MP. Visits Scandinavia, but is unsuccessful in his attempt to enter Russia.

1923-24   In Paris.

1924   Writing in Ford Madox Ford's *the transatlantic review*.

A picture of Coldside in 1928 from Ned Wilson's family album.

Nellist's
Occasional Journal

Nellist's Nautical School
10 Summerhill Terrace
Newcastle upon Tyne, 4

The cover from a copy of *Nellist's Occasional Journal.*

1924   Visits Pound in Rapallo and settles nearby.

1925   February 18 T.L. Bunting dies of 'angina pectoris'.

1925   February 21 T.L. Bunting buried in Old Jesmond Cemetery.

1925   **VILLON**—his first long poem, much admired by Pound and Eliot.

1926   Lecturing on currency at Lemington Adult School. Bunting is believed to have lived in Throckley throughout this year.

1927   Music critic for *The Outlook* and *The Town Crier,* writing regularly for a number of other magazines and newspapers.

1928   Living with Ned Wilson in the Simonsides. Bunting obviously broke his stay with Wilson with trips to London and to Throckley. Although Coldside was a relatively isolated farm it was well served by the Rothbury branch of the North British Railway which had a halt at nearby Fontburn. He seems to have spent the autumn of 1928 in the Simonsides and it would have been hard for him to ignore the Rothbury Trials of 8 October that year, which served as an informal gathering of the Northumbrian shepherds and their families.

1929   January, travels on the continent. Leaves Berlin, returns to Rapallo in the spring. Meets W.B. Yeats.

1929   Meets Marian Culver in Venice and marries her on 9 July 1930 at Riverhead, Long Island, USA.

Visits Amalfi. Preparing *Redimiculum Matellarum.*

1930   *Redimiculum Matellarum*—his first pamphlet collection—privately printed in Milan.

1931   Bourtai, (daughter) is born at Genoa, Italy.

1931   **ATTIS** and **AUS DEM ZWEITEN REICH**: two further 'sonatas'.

1934   4 February Roudaba, (second daughter) born at Santa Cruz de Tenerife.

1935   **THE WELL OF LYCOPOLIS**

1937   15 May, Rustam (son) born in Eau Claire, Wisconsin, USA.

1937-38 Sailing his boat *The Thistle* for a year.

1938   Nellist's Nautical School, Newcastle upon Tyne.

1939 Returns to Northumberland from America. Gives WEA Lectures on history.

1940 Decree absolute granted to Marian in Wisconsin.

1940 Having been rejected by the Navy and the Army, apparently on medical grounds, finally in July he is accepted in the RAF. On 21 September enlists at the RAF receiving centre at Padgate near Warrington in Cheshire (1119305 AC1 Bunting medical category A 4B—Grade II vision 27/40), he is assigned to Balloon Operations in Hull, later as mate escorting convoys with balloons, on the converted yacht *The Golden Hind*.

His Official War Record reads:

RC Padgate, 21 September 1940.

17 BC, 27 September 1940.

948 Squadron, 19 December 1940.

929 Squadron, 2 March 1942.

982 (BB) Squadron, 30 April 1942.

Iraq, 7 May 1942.

982 Squadron, Iraq, 6 August 1942.

September 1943 Iraq Com. Home Comm.

(He was discharged on 1 June 1943. During this time his rank was Aircraftsman 1 and from October 1942 Leading Aircraftsman. As early as December 1941 he was recommended for appointment to a commissioned rank in the Intelligence Branch.

On 2 June 1943 he was granted a Commission for the emergency as Pilot Officer on probation in the Administrative & Special Duties Branch of the RAF Volunteer Reserve.)

982 Squadron, 2 June 1943 Supplementary on Appointment to Commission.

Regional Headquarters, Malta, 21 June 1943. Intelligence.

229 Squadron, 4 October 1943, Intelligence.

229 Squadron, 10 April 1944, Intelligence.

Bunting rose rapidly through the ranks during this time, first as Flying Officer, then Flight Lieutenant. In January 1945 he was appointed Acting Squadron Leader. This rank was retained in April 1946. He appears to still be on the Supplementary List (Secretarial Intelligence) in August 1950 and finally relinquished his Commission still retaining the rank of Squadron Leader, on 10 February 1954.

1947-48 Assistant Counsellor at the British Embassy in Teheran with special responsibility for monitoring Persian public opinion.

1948 Meets Sima Alladadian, a Kurdo-Armenian from Isfahan. He marries her in the Embassy on 2 December. Because of his marriage he has to leave the Foreign Office, so he becomes a correspondent for *The Times*.

1949 While working as *The Times* correspondent he is acting for the Directors of the Anglo-Iranian Oil Company.

1950 February, Sima-Maria born.

1950 *Poems 1950*—his first full collection published by the Cleaners Press, Galveston, Texas.

1951-2 Again *The Times* correspondent in Teheran—expelled by Mossadeq. He returns with the family to live with his mother at 242 Newburn Road, Throckley.

1951 **THE SPOILS**—one of his first long poems—published in *Poetry (Chicago)*.

1952 Rustam dies aged 16 from polio, while away at school.

1952 November, Thomas Faramaz born.

1954 26 July, appointed as a sub-editor on the *Newcastle Daily Journal*. This period of Bunting's life is fairly obscure. He was to write in 1964 that he felt as if he had been dead for ten years and that Dante had nothing to add to the Hell that he knew from his own experience. His major diversions at this time were reading, his garden and walking.

1957 June, moves with mother to Shadingfield, Elm Bank, Wylam, Northumberland while Sima and the children are in Persia. December begins to work day-shift on the *Newcastle Evening Chronicle*.

1962 Margaret de Silver dies.

1963 Meets Jonathan Williams for the first time.

1964 June, Tom Pickard phones, then meets Bunting.

1965 *The Spoils* (Morden Tower pamphlet).

Basil Bunting: a Thomson House photograph from 1966.

Newcastle Chronicle & Journal Ltd.

Basil Bunting in Newcastle upon Tyne in the 1960s.

© David James

Basil Bunting and his longstanding friend, the American poet and photographer, Jonathan Williams at a Colpitts Poetry Reading in 1977. Richard Caddel is on the extreme right.

1965   **BRIGGFLATTS**

1965   11 June sends *Briggflatts* to *Poetry*.

1965   29 September 'Cape is doing my Collected Works next year' (letter to Dorothy Pound).

1965   November, *First Book of Odes* published by Stuart Montgomery's newly-established Fulcrum Press.

1965   December, *Loquitur* published by Fulcrum Press. Reads *Briggflatts* at Morden Tower.

1966   February, *Briggflatts* (Fulcrum Press).

1966   Arts Council Bursary for 1966.

1966   30 August, retires from the *Evening Chronicle*.

1967   Operation on one eye in California (where he was lecturing at the University of California at Santa Barbara) to remove a cataract.

1968   16 August, *Descant on Rawthey's Madrigal*, conversations with Jonathan Williams, published.

1968-70 Northern Arts Fellow in Poetry at the Universities of Durham and Newcastle.

1972   President of the Poetry Society.

1974-1977 President of Northern Arts.

1976   January *Selected Poems of Joseph Skipsey* (Ceolfrith). Skipsey's poems were an important voice for the Northumberland Miners. William Straker the Northumberland Miners General Secretary used Skipsey's *Get Up* along with moving descriptions to great effect in his account of the Montague Pit Disaster.

1977   July, living at 107 Striding Edge, Blackfell, Washington, County Durham.

1978   16 March, *Collected Poems* (Oxford University Press).

1981   May, moves to The Cottage, Greystead, Tarset, Northumberland.

1984   July, moves to Fox Cottage, Whitley Chapel, near Hexham.

1985   17 April, dies in Hexham General Hospital.

Notes

1. During his lifetime Bunting resisted formal attempts at biography, though he was prepared to talk to sympathetic interviewers about his life, and much anecdotal material has found its way into print. The present authors determined to verify as much as possible from contemporary sources, though it has to be said that much of Bunting's history still seems to resist verification! His war record is known in outline, but much of the substance of his time in the RAF and subsequently in Persia and Italy is concealed by the Official Secrets Act. What does remain is useful because it tells us what Bunting himself considered to be important and deserves to be recorded for that reason.

2. Bunting left little in the way of reminiscence about his family. This description of his father is exceptional though it still gives few hints as to their relationship. The apparent lack of interest in his paternal grandparents in Heanor is also notable, it seems that Bunting's desire to advance his Northern credentials led to his ignoring his Derbyshire connections. This seems all the more remarkable in that his father was clearly an exceptional man.

3. Dorothy Ellison, a former patient of Dr Bunting, in a conversation with the authors in 1996, recalled walking from her home in Westerhope to collect medicines from the surgery in Denton Road. The dark entrance remains in her mind, as did the wearing of rabbit skin gloves by Dr Bunting, which led her and her brothers to amend the nursery rhyme *Bye Baby Bunting* to include the words: 'Dr Bunting went a hunting'.

4. Bunting's exchange with George Renwick requires placing in context. Renwick was MP for Central Newcastle with five commissioned sons in various regiments, so that his position with regards to the War was implacably opposed to that of Bunting's. After the War in 1923, Renwick—by that time Sir George—gave a memorial to the city commemorating the raising of B Company, 9th Battalion, and the 16th, 18th and 19th Service Battalions, Northumberland Fusiliers. This 'Renwick' Memorial stands at Barras Bridge in an imposing position in front of the Civic Centre.

5. Andrew Messer was born at Hexham, Northumberland on 23 December 1866. Educated at Edinburgh and Heidelberg, he became Medical Officer of Health to Newburn Urban District Council and Senior Assistant Surgeon at the Northumberland and Durham Eye Infirmary, Medical Superintendent of the Newburn and Gosforth Joint Isolation Hospital and Member of the Incorporated Society of Medical Officers of Health. He was married to Annie Bunting's sister Elizabeth and it is to be supposed that it was Andrew Messer's friendship with Thomas Lowe Bunting that led to the latter moving from Derbyshire to settle on Tyneside. He was a man of considerable talent with a strong social conscience which informed his interest in public health and education. His son, Malcolm Messer (1901-1984) was a contemporary of Bunting's at Leighton Park, having entered the school in January 1917. He was also a journalist. Another son, Walter Messer (1895-1915) died while Bunting was at Ackworth. It is interesting to note that both Malcolm Messer and Bunting were 'short-time' Leightonians, attending for a period of six and four terms respectively, rather than the more usual five years.

6. Arthur Cook was the firebrand secretary of the Miners' Federation of Great Britain. He adopted a negotiating stance that was typified in the words: 'Not a minute on the day, not a penny off the pay'—demands which by the end of 1926 the Miners' Federation had had to concede. It is possible that Bunting was involved in the disturbances that took place on the 6 May 1926 in Throckley. A large crowd of between three and four hundred Throckley pitmen began picketing traffic on

Hexham Road, Throckley. This started at 6am and it was not until midday that police were able to break up the group and make arrests, this was not before stones had been thrown at lorries and windows broken; drivers were informed that if they attempted to cross the picket lines their lorries would be tipped over. Thirty-two men were arrested and subsequently tried under the Emergency Regulations at the Moot Hall Police Court on Tuesday 18 May 1926. It was clear that the police had been determined to apprehend 'disaffected' and 'communist agitators' and therefore break the back of the strike. Five ringleaders were imprisoned and twenty-seven others were fined five pounds.

7. Bunting's significant places are well known in the region except perhaps for the Isabella pit heap at Throckley, which is no more. The photograph of Bunting beside the Reeth, taken from a family album, locates him as a young boy at a place that was to remain of importance, even into old age. The origins of the Reeth are obscure, though it could have been formed as a result of controlled subsidence—in local mining dialect a 'goaf'—of workings from the nearby Isabella Pit. It is marked on old maps as a reservoir and it is possible that the water was used to power a steam engine at the Isabella Pit. In recent years its shape and size have been much affected by impoundment of shale from the Isabella pit heap during reclamation work. Bunting's last working notebooks include descriptions of a 'goaf', which also found its way into the last poem he was working on—*Such syllables flicker out of grass*. The most notable slag heap of the area, at nearby Newburn, was that of the Percy Pit known locally as 'The Black Alp', created as dumping ground for slag from five local collieries, which once towered an astonishing 150 feet. It is possible that it was this pit heap that Bunting was referring to.

Basil Bunting pictured at the Reeth, Throckley c.1910.

Selected Bibliography

Agenda Volume 16 No. 1: **Basil Bunting Special Issue,** Spring 1978.

Bête Noire Volume 2/3 Spring 1987.

Gordon Brown (ed.), **High on the Walls: An Anthology Celebrating Twenty-Five Years of Poetry Readings at Morden Tower**, Morden Tower in association with Bloodaxe Books 1990.

Basil Bunting, **Complete Poems** ed. Richard Caddel, Oxford University Press 1994.

Basil Bunting: **An Historic Series of Poetry Readings, Lectures and Interviews Recorded by the Poet between 1967 and 1984** (Eight Audio Cassettes), Richard Swigg (ed.), Keele University in association with The Basil Bunting Poetry Centre, Durham 1992.

Basil Bunting, **A Note on Briggflatts,** Basil Bunting Poetry Centre, Durham 1989.

Richard Caddel, 'Acknowledged Land', A Biography of *They Say Etna* and a Debate between Bunting and Pound in **Ezra Pound and Europe** ed. by Richard Taylor and Claus Melchior, Rodopi; Amsterdam, 1993**.**

Richard Caddel (ed.), **Sharp Study and Long Toil,** Special Edition of the Durham University Journal, 1995.

Conjunctions 8, New York 1985.

J. Davison, **Northumberland Miners 1919-1939,** Co-operative Press Ltd. 1973.

Victoria Forde, **The Poetry of Basil Bunting,** Bloodaxe 1991.

Nina Hamnett, **Laughing Torso,** Constable 1932.

Percy A. Lovell, 'The Musicians' in **Lit and Phil Bicentenary Lectures** 1993.

Peter Makin, **Bunting: The Shaping of his Verse**. Oxford University Press 1992.

F.C. Moffatt, **'A Tap at the End of the Raa'** Volume 3 (Collieries Near the Tyne), Morpeth Northumberland no date.

Montemora 3, Spring 1977.

Paideuma Volume 9 No.1, Spring 1980.

Connie Pickard, 'Basil Bunting 1900-1985: a personal memoir' in *Stand,* Volume 26, No. 3 1985.

Poetry Information Volume 19**,** ed. Peter Hodgkiss Autumn 1978.

Peter Quartermain, **Basil Bunting: Poet of the North,** Basil Bunting Poetry Centre Durham 1990.

N.G. Rippeth, **Newburn in Old Picture Postcards,** European Library—Zaltbommel/Netherlands 1993**.**

R. Murray Schafer (ed.), **Ezra Pound and Music,** Faber 1978.

Noel Stock, **The Life of Ezra Pound,** Penguin Books 1974**.**

Carroll F. Terrell, (ed.), **Basil Bunting Man and Poet,** ed. The National Poetry Foundation Maine 1980.

Jonathan Williams, **Descant on Rawthey's Madrigal,** Gnomon Press, Kentucky 1968.

Bill Williamson, **Class, Culture and Community**, Routledge and Kegan Paul 1982.

Last but not least acknowledgment must be made to the excellent local history publications of Newcastle City Libraries which have provided the authors with much valuable background information.